THE RACING BREED

by
Helen Ueltzen

illustrations
by

FREDERICK FELL PUBLISHERS
NEW YORK

GFI Associates
Middleburg, Virginia 22117

Library of Congress Cataloging in Publication Data

Ueltzen, Helen, 1946–
  The racing breed.

1. Horse-racing.   2. Race horses.   3. Thoroughbred
horse.   I. Title.
SF334.U35   1983   798.4   83-20706
ISBN 0-915309-00-9

Distributed By:
FREDERICK FELL PUBLISHERS, INC.
386 Park Avenue South • New York, N.Y. 10016
ISBN 0-8119-0694-9

Printed in the United States of America
Color separations by ISCOA (International Scanner Corporation of America)
5801 Lee Highway, Arlington, Virginia 22207

TO MIKE—

This is the book you would have written, if only there had been enough time between flights to the jungles of Brunei and the deserts of Africa. You were pursuing what you do best: making money.

Edward H. Flint, National President
Horsemen's Benevolent & Protective Association

"*THE RACING BREED* is one of those rare books—informative, absorbing, yet easy to read and understand. It really captures the essense and exuberance of the world of Thoroughbred racing.

"I studied the manuscript with great interest, and I believe it will serve as an excellent introduction to the sport for new fans.

"I advise those people just coming into the business, or thinking about 'taking the plunge,' to read this book. They will be much more knowledgeable and better prepared as horsemen for having done so. The chapters concerning horse care, how to choose a trainer, and the financial responsibilities of running a horse in particular will be of great assistance to owners.

"Ms. Ueltzen's breezy and candid style made *THE RACING BREED* a pleasure for me to read. And the heart-warming vignettes sprinkled throughout the book help to remind all of us why we became involved in racing in the first place—for the sheer pleasure of it!"

Robert Brennan, Chairman of the Board
International Thoroughbred Breeders, Inc.
Garden State Park and Keystone Race Track

"My advice to all new owners in Thoroughbred racing is to save the blinkers for your horse. *THE RACING BREED* will give you a good look at the world of racing so that you'll understand right from the start about the great demands of the sport.

"You need to know what racing will entail in terms of emotional, as well as financial, expenditures. Any failure on the track is highly visible, just as your successes may bring you instant recognition. The sword cuts both ways.

"Owning racehorses represents one of the most intriguing challenges in the modern business world. That's why you've got to go into racing fortified with knowledge and the right attitude. Plan on uncertainty, and stock up on staying power."

ACKNOWLEDGEMENTS

The entire racetrack community lent a hand in writing *THE RACING BREED*. It educated and inspired. Outside the sport, others have encouraged me by their fascination with the subject. A heartfelt thanks to all of you, particularly:

Barbara Baird
Terence Collier, Fasig-Tipton
Lee Couchenour
Julie A. Day
Michael P. Sandler, *DAILY RACING FORM*
Burt Fagan
J. Wm. Henry
Kim Herbert, *THE BLOOD-HORSE*
Don Hudson and Bill McDonald
Cindi Whitcomb, Horsemen's Benevolent & Protective Association
Sam Kanchuger, The Jockey Club
Joe Kelly, Laurel Race Course
Michael Kelly, The Irish Sage
Chick Lang, General Manager, Pimlico Race Course
The Maryland Horse Breeders Association
W.H. McCormick, V.M.D.
Col. Muggins, Bowie Race Course
Andy Narel
Lou Raffetto and staff, Laurel Race Course and Monmouth Park
Scott Regan
Aylett Simpson, *THE THOROUGHBRED RECORD*
Bill Solomon, V.M.D.
Jack Killion, Thoroughbred Development Corporation of New Jersey
Gudrun Ueltzen
Holmes Marshall Wagoner III

PREFACE

Racing takes money. But having money is relative. If you have millions at your disposal or a genes pool of Thoroughbred breeding stock spinning off stakes-level horses, go with it. On the other hand, if you have a well-established income and it gives you enough money to have fun with every year, this book is for you. As long as you want to be master of your own stable and not a fragment of a syndicate, very little "how-to" information is directed to you. You are not what the commercial breeders and large scale wheeler-dealers are looking for. And yet you will always be the backbone of a solid racing industry.

THE
RACING CARD

Chapter One

FUNDAMENTALS

Chapter Two

ORGANIZATION

Chapter Three

LIFESPAN

Chapter Four

TRAITS

Chapter Five

BUYER BEWARE

Chapter Six

TRACKBOUND

Chapter Seven

CAN YOU MANAGE?

Chapter Eight

SURVIVAL

APPENDICES

CREDITS

FUNDAMENTALS

Racing is like religion. It can be a spectacle, a gamble or a quest to find valiance in the slipshod modern world. Whatever you are looking for, a winning horse might just give you all that you hope to find.

Horseracing is as ruthless as it is addictive. Behind the razzle-dazzle, the millionaire auctions and the social season, you'll find the real-life sport of Thoroughbred racing. Few horsemen get fat. They face an underlying struggle to wrestle down expenses and reverses, despite the glory days.

Go into racing with your eyes open. Most newly licensed owners are successful people who smugly assume that racing will be a pleasant sideline, generating satisfaction and profits just as their other ventures have so gratefully done. They'll find out the hard way that understanding and toughness go farther than the Midas touch in earning the reward of a runner.

THE RACING BREED will course through a landscape of racetracks, farms and auctions to give you the smell and the feel of the real thing. You should end up knowing enough to ask some good questions when talking shop with other horsemen. Watch your step, though, because anybody who has ever been right once in racing considers himself an expert. Ignorance is rampant. That's why you must ultimately build your own mosaic of knowledge out of the general clamor of advice and the unforgiving onslaught of racing experience.

This is a beginning. Racing's story will change more in the next few years than it has in the last one hundred. Training technique and vet procedures are under assault from the modern world because, with prices soaring for racing stock, investors can be forgiven for expecting their horses to last. It's time for space-age science to lend racing a hand, even though track whimsy and tradition will always be strong.

Horses don't win many races on a wish and a prayer. If you give them good horsemanship and smart management, they won't surprise—they'll perform. And you will win.

POST TIME

Introducing hardcore fans to racing is like telling them that a horse has four legs. Even so, there are plenty of people in the outside world could use some background to help them understand the ins and outs of the sport. They should start at the track and make it their second home.

Everyone finds a niche. You'll always see a few die-hard horseplayers who'd begrudge any dollar not pushed through the window. For them, an odds board in a bullpit ripe with hot dogs, smoke and body sweat could be just this side of heaven. Still others love the good life as much as the gamble, and go for the visual charm and comforts of racing.

Betting fans of every intensity are the sport's bread and butter. But what often happens is that as you get closer to the horses, the urgency of betting starts to dwindle. Horses become a source of fascination in and of themselves. They are the ultimate gamble, the ultimate challenge. Most racehorse owners live to win, not to pull a betting coup.

Racetracks have a carnival side and their grounds overflow with hucksters, clowns and fortune-tellers. The trouble is, new owners stand first in line to get taken for every ride. That's why it's good to go close to the action to learn the ropes. You'll want to see your horse saddled and talk to the jock; catch him again hot off the horse, before he finds time to dream up a line. Let yourself drift with the crowd like the tide from paddock to window to rail, and back again. You'll be mesmerized by the pageantry and transported to a world far removed from this century.

Ritual

The typical race-day card holds nine races with about half an hour leading up to each race. Start your tour at the paddock, where the horses are led in by their solemn grooms for saddling. You'll feel tension stir the air as the trainers, owners and ragtag begin to mill there, uneasy with their burdens of speculation and hope. Before long, the jockeys will saunter in and eye their mounts while they half-listen to the earnest instructions coming from all sides.

A flourish of recorded trumpets breaks over the loudspeaker to announce the post parade back onto the track. This is the signal for each jock to look to the trainer for a leg-up and shove so that he can scramble aboard without a stepladder. He'll nod to the catcalls and start to unravel the mane braids for a better hold, balancing easy as his racehorse swirls and bounds alongside a lead pony. They'll jog and they'll canter, and arrive at the gate well warmed up and on the muscle.

Invisible clothespin clamped firmly into place, the race caller twangs, "It is *now* post time."

Hair stands on end, binoculars are focused and the racers are loaded into the starting gate. This unwieldy device is handily operated by the starting gate crew, who often go so far as to "tail" (hold by the tail) a reluctant starter to keep him from sitting down. Reform school types can even get their ears or noses pinned with a pair of tongs which pretty well ensures a safe, but slow, start. So you ought to know you're witnessing a miracle every time young horses go right up to the gate, load calmly and wait with easy patience for the doors to spring open.

A race can last many lifetimes for the heavy bettor or the connections of an expensive first-time starter, but it's actually over so fast that watching the videotape replay is the only way to absorb all the nuances. The toteboard will light up with the results, running time and parimutuel betting pay-offs, while the winner's entourage gets a chance to crow and have its picture taken. All the jockeys are routinely weighed out just to make sure they haven't dropped off the lead from their saddles behind the far bushes.

Tired horses amble off to get cleaned up and cooled down. The steaming winner and often another starter chosen at random will first have to visit the "spit barn" (test barn) for the official drug check of saliva, blood or urine. Racehorses have been taught to urinate there at the sound of a groom's whistle, the last word in saving time.

Programs

The programs hawked at the track provide basic information about each race. There can actually be two types of programs, the traditional palm-fitting version and the newer one designed along the lines of a junior *RACING FORM*, complete with past performance data on each horse. Although tracks outdo themselves to make both programs self-explanatory, a couple of lines of detail help round out the picture.

You'll find, for example, race distance designated in furlongs (a "furrow long") which equal an eighth of a mile. "Par" running time for a furlong is 12 seconds so that a six furlong race run in one minute and 12 seconds would be a decent time, although several seconds slower than the track record printed on the program.

The privilege of being named as owner, and bill-payer, is taken on by applying for an annual license. State racing commissions maintain offices for this purpose at every racetrack. The licensing procedure was originally designed as a way to keep crooks out of the sport, but it has turned out to be a handy source of money for most state racing commissions. Just about everybody connected with the track needs a license, and trainers have to qualify with a one-time written and practical test.

The owner designs his own colors described in the program. In most states, they are automatically registered on the standard license application form. Any tack shop should have these silks sewn up for you in a week or two so that you can hand them right over to the track colors man who will see that they are kept laundered and trotted out for the jockey on race-day.

A jockey is named for each mount by the trainer, hopefully with some input from the owner. Most trainers would like to enter into a long-term relationship with a particular rider, while others prefer matching jocks to each horse's running style. Either way, trainers want to steer clear of "mucksacks," jockeys who are perennially overweight. The constant dieting, sweating and vomiting are bound to sap their strength.

The value of a crafty and aggressive jockey is agonizingly clear to anyone who has seen a horse's best efforts foiled by incompetency. What you need is a pilot, not a passenger. But a horse isn't an F-16, and his jockey can't just push a pedal and expect instant acceleration. Horses can be perverse beasts and the best hands in the business don't help much if a horse won't fire. That's why a completely honest horse who never sulks or loafs is a wonderous thing! No one has been able to figure out how to breed in that magical ingredient called heart which will keep some horses running long after their ability runs out.

The Claiming Game

There are three basic types of races—claiming, allowance and stakes races—plus a handful of hybrids to keep things interesting. Claiming races are the most plentiful on the card while the least prestigious. Every horse in a particular claiming race is for sale at the same basic price, which ensures that all the starters are pretty evenly matched in racing worth.

A horse's "connections," meaning his trainer and owner, decide which claiming level he will be racing on. It's a subjective decision and involves weighing a horse's talent, soundness and heart against the quality of horses found at each level. The idea is to find a race on a level where the horse can handle the competition. Go too high and your horse doesn't stand a chance; go too low and that horse may win easily but will probably be claimed (bought) by another horseman for less than he is worth. Claiming is capitalism's way of keeping the competition fair.

Claiming prices can range from a rockbottom $1500 at bush league ovals all the way up to $100,000 and more at the big league tracks. The Racing Secretary at each track schedules claiming races on the variety of levels which he feels reflects the composition of horses stabled on the grounds. These are written up in a condition book covering a couple of weeks' worth of racing days so that a horseman has plenty of time to study the options open to his horses, not only in claiming level but in length and type of race. Some claiming races are restricted to female horses, others have age specifications and so on.

Any horseman who submits a claim slip to buy a certain horse must be prepared to halter that horse right after the race regardless of how the horse acquitted himself (as long as he started through the gate). If the winning horse is claimed, the purse goes to the original owner. That owner may consider losing his horse as a slap on the wrist for running the horse on too easy a level or as a handy way to conduct the business of selling horses.

The appeal of claiming a horse is that you can acquire a ready-made race-horse on the spot that can most likely be sent out again in two weeks' time to earn money under your own banner. The claimed animal hardly ever develops into a world-beater, but is usually a proven entity with the ability to stimulate an immediate and positive cash flow. This garden variety "plater"—so called because some say he is only worth as much as the racing plates on his feet—has kept many a stable solvent while waiting for its dream horse to come to hand. With luck, Wonderhorse will eventually be ready to take his place among the elite in allowance and stakes races, where the money is big and talent is balanced through weights and conditions. Or, he may flop.

DAILY RACING FORM

The serious handicapper's sine qua non is the *RACING FORM* on sale at every track entrance and well-stocked newsstand. No doubt fortunes have been made betting on the prettiest horse or the wildest hunch but if you really want to understand what's going on in racing, read it.

©*DAILY RACING FORM*

The "telegraph," as the cognoscenti call it, carries the news, scuttlebutt and essential racing statistics of several tracks in each of its geographic editions. The rundown of the race card—who's favored in what and why—is shrewd guesswork similar to what you'd find on racing in the sports section of any good newspaper. The *FORM's* fortune is its "Past Performances." Drawing on a mammoth computerized memory bank, the *FORM* paints an uncannily accurate picture of every starter's last few races. Each past performance is synthesized for history into one line of closely packed minutiae. A glance will tell you the date, place, distance, speed, level, trip, rider and results in addition to some more esoteric considerations.

Racetrack aficionados can, and owners must, become adept at interpreting and retaining past performance information. Since the typical racehorse runs for several months at regular two-week intervals, there are some railbirds who manage to carry around in their heads a current performance index of all the local platers.

The most enterprising horsemen compute—or buy—speed figures, a tedious but rewarding way of comparing racing skill. These figures go a mile further than the *FORM'S* calculations in boiling down the conditions which might have helped or hindered a runner's timed speed in order to grade his talent accurately. Handicapping's wizard, Andy Beyer of *THE WASHINGTON POST*, deserves credit for refining and popularizing this process to the extent that it sounds the death knell for the hardboot homily, "Time only counts when you're in prison."

The weighing of so many variables is why racetrack handicapping has been called the most intellectual form of gambling. While most horsemen would argue that it's simplistic to summarize a race with a few key statistics, horsemen will also admit in the same breath that they've been luckier at the betting window and claiming booth when they've analyzed the *RACING FORM* statistics instead of relying on memory or rumor. The *FORM* provides an objective measuring stick in an otherwise highly subjective sport.

Track Variants

The patterns perceived in the *RACING FORM* about a horse's racing style, and whether he likes a fast or slow track, wet or dry, still have to be applied to the track conditions of the day. These are stated on the toteboard but never with the right degree of accuracy. It's up to the individual handicapper to keep a close eye on the times and observe how each race is run. There are only a few well-loved horses who can adjust their running styles to varying track conditions. Most fall into a groove.

The "closer" enjoys lagging behind the pace, being relaxed or "rated" until it's time to make his move and overtake the leaders. This tactic works well on a heavy, tiring racetrack where the going is so laborious that speedballs wear themselves out in short order. A track advantageous to closers might be in a sandy, deep or mucky state.

At the other extreme, "speed" horses—those that like to break on top and run in front, wire to wire—will excel on a hard, fast track which can occur if the ground is frozen or beaten down. A track that is extremely wet and sloppy so that water pools on the top of a packed surface is also considered speed-favoring. Arguments rage over whether this results from a property of the wet track itself or from the spray which works to demoralize the trailing horses.

It's easy to see how the old-time designation of "mudder" can be confusing since mud will turn up fast or slow, slick or gunky, depending on the degree of wetness. The complexion of the mud usually determines how well a horse will be able to handle an "off-track" in keeping with his style of running. But you will always find a few true mudders who seem to have inherited the joy of splashing, along with a physique for it. It's also a good bet that a horse with concussion injuries in his feet, joints or bones might well appreciate a soft and muddy landing strip.

JUST DUCKY

Hidden Pool. It didn't take long to guess his game from his name. He loved water. Any kind of wet track would do. Even the kind of muck that would suck the shoes right off your feet.

Pool was skinny and greyhound fast. While others floundered, he skimmed. Hugged the rail tight and dove through holes, which were left open wide as the big guys skidded and spun around the tight turns.

Despite the ouches of age and a screw in his leg. Hidden Pool was running in form. Won seven nice ones. Had a wonderful time: it rained.

©DAILY RACING FORM

'HAVING FUN ?'

Even though track surfaces can change dramatically with inclement weather, most will quickly spring back into their distinctive personalities. Around Miami, Gulfstream is famous as a lightning-fast track, while Calder's surfaces are snail-slow in contrast. It's still not uncommon for a bias to appear within these tracks from time to time to distort the forecasts and promise a windfall to bettors who recognize it early. For instance, the rail might show signs of becoming a paved roadway in contrast to the depth of the other lanes or vice versa. Today, thanks to assiduous maintenance crews, tracks will sometimes turn up completely fair or "even", creating universal puzzlement and disbelief.

Special attention to track construction and upkeep is catching on as a way of preventing injuries caused by a lumpy cushion or uneven surface and the havoc wrought by extreme weather. Even under the best conditions, though, it's axiomatic that racing takes its toll on Thoroughbreds. Their body weight seems disproportionate to their slender legs which take an incredible pounding at high speed. Injuries are an ever-present possibility and can contribute heavily to wayward luck in racing. Undetected soreness will throw any odds-on favorite off form.

Don't let the injury factor spoil racing for you. It is there with any athlete, horse or human, who extends himself to the limits of his capabilities. The key function of the racehorse trainer, who is more appropriately called a "conditioner," is to keep his animals healthy, sound and fit enough to run to their potential. A visit to the backstretch facilities of any competent trainer will convince you that the typical racehorse gets a generous share of attention and coddling in a labor-intensive environment. The main thrust of the Thoroughbred industry is that if you don't care for your horses, you can't count on their earnings.

Racing is natural. Even young horses on the farm will shoot pell-mell from one end of the field to the other, one race after another, during the course of a day's play. Some have more ability and some more aggression, but the Thoroughbred on the whole is custom-built for ethereal running grace and power. And this is showcased for us in the racetracks of the world.

WORLDWIDE RACING

Like surfers looking for the perfect wave, horsemen can travel the world over to indulge in their passion for the sport. Shared enthusiasm makes up for vagaries of custom and speech. All racetrackers speak their own special brand of Esperanto, the language of hope.

Great Britain

U.S. racing is the spiritual child of England. Charles II is more or less credited with siring modern racing during his reign from 1660–85. He burst into Newmarket, hopped aboard mounts and dangled carrots to all comers in the form of silver racing prizes which became known as King's Plates. By 1752, Britain's Jockey Club was set up, and in 1791 Weatherby's General Stud Book hit the book stands. About this same time, handicapping was invented as a way of equalizing competition by assigning different weights for each horse to carry in a particular race.

The Thoroughbred as we know it sprang from the matings of England's best mares with a handful of Arab stallions imported around 1700. For years Britons strictly defined a Thoroughbred as a horse who could trace his male line back to the Byerly Turk, Darley's Arabian or the Godolphin Barb.

Today there are a lot of little differences between racing in England and in the United States. Just as we drive on the right and they stick to the left, many English races run clockwise and—you guessed it—we go around to the left. Racetracks in England are highly individual, most taking the rough shape of a hilly dogleg. English meets are shorter and racing less frequent, probably because all racing is done on the turf which in spite of (or because of) England's rain takes a whale of a beating. The flat-racing season traditionally runs from March to November, when the braver steeplechase crowd jumps in. Even so, duck weather during the regular racing season can bring its share of cancellations.

Grass lasts better with races that are longer and accordingly slower, forestalling the storm of divots which would be kicked up in the hustle-bustle of a sprint. In a typical English race, the horses lope around for much of an eternity; only when heading for the barn do things seem to pick up. By that time, the crowd is more or less asleep which is why you get the impression nobody watches the races. In fact, flat-racing can be a downright bore compared to the murderous steeplechases which England made famous.

English jumping races are highly popular with the fans. U.S. racetracks also used to card steeplechases on a routine basis, but the practice has largely died out because of the high cost of upkeep and the lack of betting interest. There was a visceral feeling among bettors that jumping races were fielded with horses from a different world and smacked too much of gentlemanly privilege and a dilettante style.

Since most off-track jumping race meets ("hunt races") in the U.S. do not offer parimutuel betting, they have had to become the realm of passionately devoted sportsmen. The knocks are hard and the purses small. The meets are scattered on weekends throughout the spring and fall, and draw boisterous fair weather crowds. People show up in pick-ups and Rolls Royces, with their picnic baskets or liveried tailgate parties.

Back to the track: Britons have often complained that U.S. flat-racing is nasty and brutish. It's true that a campaign in England may be more pleasant for the horse. Horses there are stabled at "yards" near racing centers which share country-like "gallops." Even if sound, they race infrequently, and warm up well when running. Speed is spread out more evenly over the race with smart positioning for a final kick being the good part of a win. Fine aristocratic pacing prompts English jockeys to ride so high that they must shove their cap visors up like bonnets to get a better view. This touch of elegance contrasts with the aerodynamics, guts and hustle of the American street-fighter style.

English racing is built on an everyday diet of allowance and handicap races, with an occasional selling race, where the winner is up for grabs. Our own dollar-sign system uses claiming races to determine the worth and talent level of the majority of racehorses. Since most trainers would prefer to run their horses in easy competition on the lower levels, claiming races keep U.S. horsemen part-way honest because they run the risk of losing a horse that's spotted too cheap. Few such risks occur in the British system. The temptation could be sweet to cheat and pull a horse, so that he would qualify for a lower level where he might easily win and pay off a good bet to boot.

Betting in England is an interesting amalgam of the old and the new. Independent bookies and house betting coexist peaceably, while in the States only the house is legally sanctified. The house betting system, known as parimutuel betting, was actually developed in France and constitutes a system where all the bettors bet in a pool against each other. In contrast, bookmakers actually bet against the bettor. The attractive point here is that the odds given at the time you bet remain the same at pay-off time, although bookmakers may set limits to protect themselves against bankruptcy. Parimutuel odds are more fickle. They can change wildly in response to betting trends right up until post time. Computers rush data to the horseplayers who stay glued to the odds board just in case last minute signs of a betting coup crop up, with dramatic amounts being bet on a colorless choice.

Incidentally, a purely American betting scheme once enjoyed a short spell of popularity born of necessity, but never made inroads into the Thoroughbred establishment here or abroad because of the obvious risks for both bettors and bookmakers. Western dirt track racing a few years back was mostly in the form of match races, one horse against the other, which made "blanket betting" a natural. The bets were laid out on a blanket until once too often someone took off with the blanket, bets and all, as soon as the crowd turned to the rail to watch the ponies run.

BLACK GOLD

Port of Spain, Trinidad. The Brits built a rambling city around a savannah park and, dead center, they laid out the racetrack. Horses were shipped in from all over the Caribbean, but Bajan horses (from Barbados) and home-grown Portegee jocks reigned supreme.

Frederick was no slouch. A houseboy with vision, he took the job because the villa sprawled down the mountainside overlooking the track. Frederick could hang out on any of its terraces, hidden by bushes of frangipani and bougainvillaea, and train his field glasses on the starting gate.

Frederick's preoccupation was pervasive. The only presents he didn't hock were jars of pickles to dream on every night, but the visions of toteboards never appeared. Rock bottom. Lost out on the horses; got taken in the infield shell games. Pickpockets stole what was left of his wad. It was time to forsake the track.

Frederick grew efficient. And as dour as a Puritan elder. I missed his dirge-like singing and the whinney of his thrown-back laugh.

"For God's sake, Frederick, go back to the races. What's life for anyway?"

"Yes, Mistress," he nodded, with unusual respect, and disappeared into a pirate taxi for the jolting ride down to the land of promise.

Around the World

England's system set the stage for racetracks throughout the world, particularly in Ireland and the former colonies. As such, Australia, New Zealand and South Africa are punter's paradise.

Largely through the efforts of E.P. Taylor, daddy of long-time top sire Northern Dancer, Canadian racing is not to be sneezed at. Horses love the cooler climate and, while there's no official "white" ice racing of the type you'll find in the fashionable Swiss alpine resort of St. Moritz, the quality is exciting and the set-up professional. The great jockeys, Sandy Hawley and Jeff Fell, originally rode out of the frozen north to stake their reputations on the ice water in their veins.

Mexican horsemen seemed to enjoy Maryland racing. In this early simulcasting initiative, international broadcasting and betting has proven to be more than a gimmick. Success credits the fact that Latin American tracks resemble those in the U.S. to a large extent. There has even been a top woman jockey in Argentina, a land of machismo.

Argentina can also be counted on to produce a particularly good racehorse. These horses are typically big, randy racers who are used to extremely vigorous training. Even so, U.S. horsemen have found that imported Argentine stock needs almost a year off to become acclimatized. What's more, the reversed breeding season south of the equator means that Argentine horses will be some six months younger than their competition during the important two- and three-year-old seasons. After that, it's open company and age makes little difference. Despite these drawbacks, U.S. buyers continue to forage throughout Latin America for bargain horses. They don't come a penny a pound anywhere anymore, but a favorable exchange rate does what it can to keep the prices slashed.

Racing is a class act throughout Europe, and even the Eastern Bloc countries have started to resurrect their pre-war racehorse industries. France remains the featured star on the continent, with Parisian racing reaching levels of haute couture. Could the popularity of racing in France have anything to do with a Frenchman's appetite for horseflesh?

Nowhere, though, is gambling hysteria as strong as in the Far East. Jam-packed attendance and the resulting handle in Hong Kong are legendary. The purse structure is so nice that the Hong Kong Jockey Club actually has to restrict the privilege of horse ownership. It is considered a lucrative investment opportunity where owners stand to make an impressive profit on any old moth-bitten mount.

Japanese racing has been symbolized in this country by the horses it sends to the International Race run at Laurel Race Course each autumn. At one time you could easily pinpoint the Japanese horses on the backstretch by their strangely sci-fi ear hats. (Worn against noise, flies or nippy weather?) Horses from Japan were usually the first foreign competitors to arrive on the grounds, as the old joke goes, and the last over the finish line. This caused trackmen to grumble that horsemanship does not seem to be an indigenous Japanese trait, especially since U.S. horses have been able to walk away with top honors in Japan-based races. But the race card's not over—don't run for your car. Japanese horsemen are likely to become a world power in racing, as in all else, by dint of their determination and yen for glory.

The Arab Input

The heady foundations for possibly the world's mightiest stables are now being built by the same Arabs whose ancestors gave impetus to this preoccupation with equine speed when they let some of their tough and fast little stallions be exported to Europe a few centuries ago.

The Prophet Mohammed was big on horses and they were invaluable in his conquests. He laid down the law. That you must not abuse your horse. You should not tie him up around the neck, but instead hobble him by the hind leg. What's more, every kernel of grain given to your horse would be registered with Allah as a good deed.

His followers took to these rules easily and even went so far as to welcome horses into their tents and treat them like kin. Few Arabs could ever be tempted to sell a precious mare from a horse harem, and as for gelding a stallion, the thought doesn't exist. There is no such word. Just showing a horse with his tail not raised would be considered a cutting insult.

American commercial breeders welcomed Arab interests with open arms and slept better at night knowing that the grand old racing industry had been given new and wealthy champions. Arabs could be counted on to go first class and pay top dollar for stock, making every auction consignor dream of having two Arabs enter into a bidding contest over his horse.

'I'D RATHER BE BACK AT SARATOGA!'

©DAILY RACING FORM

Although the Arabs have at times single-handedly supported the carriage-trade breeding industry, the impact of these expensive purchases is rarely felt to the detriment of normal horsemen. Arab horses are destined for higher purposes than to compete with workaday racing stock. The Arabs have ended up putting good money into the system without taking much out of it. Still, it's ironic that they have had to indulge their racing passion primarily outside their own countries because the crux of the sport, wagering, is a Muslim sin.

It might not rate an *ENQUIRER* headline, but equine news has been filled with tales of U.S. horses surging over the globe to dominate world-class racing. Some 45,000 Thoroughbred foals born in this country in one year naturally dwarf the output of all other nations. Plenty of Yankee know-how and money are being plowed into breeding and as long as there is good coin to be made, U.S. breeders will retain their edge. Wherever you wander, you'll see American bloodlines winning races.

Locations of North American Thoroughbred Tracks

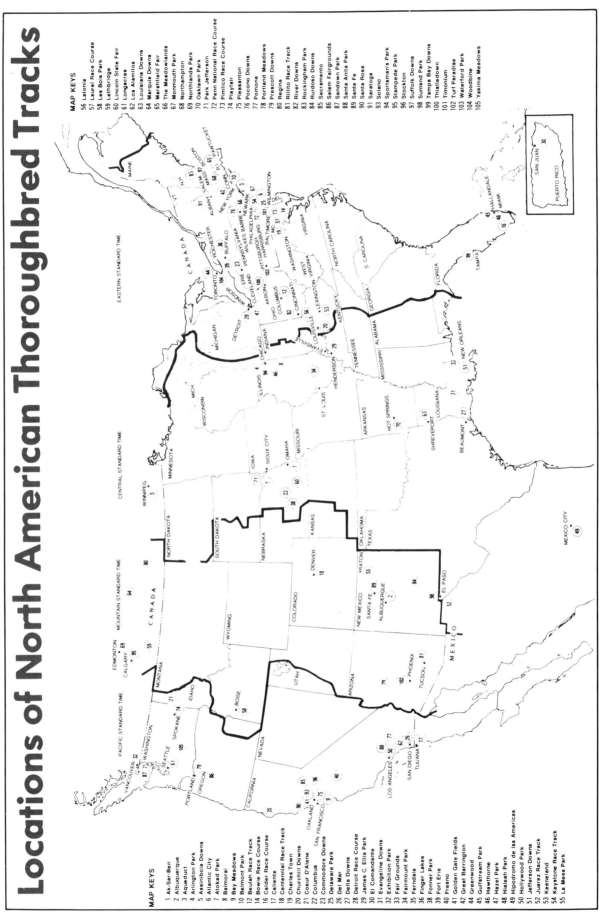

MAP KEYS

1 Ak-Sar-Ben
2 Albuquerque
3 Aqueduct
4 Arlington Park
5 Assiniboia Downs
6 Atlantic City
7 Atokad Park
8 Balmoral
9 Bay Meadows
10 Belmont Park
12 Beulah Race Track
14 Bowie Race Course
16 Calder Race Course
17 Caliente
18 Centennial Race Track
19 Charles Town
20 Coeur D'Alene
21 Columbus
22 Commodore Downs
23 Commodore Downs
24 Delaware Park
25 Del Mar
26 Del Mar
27 Delta Downs
28 Detroit Race Course
29 James C. Ellis Park
30 El Comandante
31 Evangeline Downs
32 Exhibition Park
33 Fair Grounds
34 Fairmount Park
35 Ferndale
36 Finger Lakes
38 Former Park
39 Fort Erie
40 Fresno
41 Golden Gate Fields
42 Great Barrington
44 Greenwood
45 Gulfstream Park
46 Hawthorne
47 Hazel Park
48 Hialeah Park
49 Hipodromo de las Americas
50 Hollywood Park
51 Jefferson Downs
52 Juarez Race Track
53 Keeneland
54 Keystone Race Track
55 La Mesa Park

56 Latonia
57 Laurel Race Course
58 Les Bois Park
59 Lethbridge
60 Lincoln State Fair
61 Longacres
62 Los Alamitos
63 Louisiana Downs
64 Marquis Downs
65 Marshfield Fair
66 The Meadowlands
67 Monmouth Park
68 Northampton
69 Northlands Park
70 Oaklawn Park
71 Park Jefferson
72 Penn National Race Course
73 Pimlico Race Course
74 Playfair
75 Pleasanton
76 Pocono Downs
77 Pomona
78 Portland Meadows
79 Prescott Downs
80 Regina
81 Rillito Race Track
82 River Downs
83 Rockingham Park
84 Ruidoso Downs
85 Sacramento
86 Salem Fairgrounds
87 Sandown Park
88 Santa Anita Park
89 Sante Fe
90 Santa Rosa
91 Saratoga
93 Solano
94 Sportsman's Park
95 Stampede Park
96 Stockton
97 Suffolk Downs
98 Sunland Park
99 Tampa Bay Downs
100 Thistledown
101 Timonium
102 Turf Paradise
103 Waterford Park
104 Woodbine
105 Yakima Meadows

Stateside

It's easy to be convinced that U.S. tracks hold the lead in trying to give the racing public what it wants and more. Racing has been the top spectator sport here for years, bravely surviving a proliferation of competing pastimes. Racetracks are learning to accommodate an ever-widening spectrum of pocketbook and taste as they go after the gambling dollar. They put on a show.

Most states where racing is legal have both mile and half-mile tracks. "Half-mile" is more of a designation than a description: these tracks may be merely casual or countrified, if not actually smaller. It's their purse structure that's pip-squeak. Because everything about racing is highly individual, set-ups vary from state to state, track to track. (See Appendix.)

Mile tracks in general are considered the varsity squad, but even so, there are substantial class level differences among the milers just up and down the East Coast. The rule of thumb is that the closer you go to the prestigious New York circuit, the higher the purses. You can be sure that backstretch expenses will soar in unison.

Regional and cosmetic differences also contribute to making each racetrack distinctive, if only to make it harder to decide which ones are best. Sample some.

Down South. **Florida** racing is a great spectator sport. The main Thoroughbred tracks in the Miami area are Hialeah, Calder and Gulfstream. Their grounds are lush with flowers, amenities and stalking flamingoes. The year-round calibre of horses is supported by a prolific breeding industry centered in Ocala. The word is that Florida-breds habitually outrun their pedigrees. Breeders attribute their success to the limestone soil and water, the climate and the lack of a state income tax.

You'd expect that Florida's built-in clientele of prosperous retirees and tourists would make the tracks thrive, but burgeoning competition from harness and Quarter Horse racing, dog tracks, jai-lai and traditional sports events cuts deep into the gambling pie. Not to mention the drawing power of the short hop to Caribbean casinos.

Horsemen often face drawbacks in shipping to Miami for the winter. The seasonal crush can obliterate the lure of good weather. Fields may be standing room only, with a long list of horses shut out of each race. Despite the high class competition, purses have been threadbare, though improving.

Let's face it, it's the horsemen who go for the sunshine. Horses are cold-weather creatures who stand to suffer from the tropical blahs. Backstretch wisdom will tell you that for every horse that ships south, one gets sick.

Although Miami is traditionally the place to be in January, **Louisiana**'s racing scene is coming on strong. Support for state-bred horses is so powerful that races restricted to Louisiana-breds are carded each and every day with fat stakes races often scheduled to run once a week. Louisiana's foal crop is teeming, bred with the promise that the speed horse will be king. But every now and then, there are those in the state who pause mid-step to wonder if the program isn't giving away the shop.

Mid–Atlantic. Racing in **Maryland** is old and tradition-bound, and lovely Pimlico is known as the home of the Preakness, second jewel in the Triple Crown. It has inspired Laurel, Bowie and little Timonium to brush up their no-frills, work-a-day images. Beautification programs have added charm for the spectators and comfort for the backstretch rabble. Some tracks even maintain low-cost housing for stable help in an attempt to make life less of a poverty-line struggle.

The gypsy camp patina of any backstretch is hard to dissolve, but management has struggled valiantly with barrels of paint and rewards for the best-kept shedrow. It's a whimsical battle. Shedrows everywhere have a poignant tendency to drift into shanty towns with cats, goats and roosters frisking among the drying leg wraps, while fragrant manure piles wait to be trundled off by the mushroom growers.

All around Baltimore, you'll find the ancestral homes of Maryland's finest racing families, with illustrious bloodlines rivaling those of their horses. Maryland also has less grandiose stud farms scattered liberally throughout the state and probably the highest concentration of masterful trainers found anywhere in the United States.

West Virginia racing specializes in half-mile tracks, strictly country. Cowboy hats and baseball caps may be de rigueur, but the public facilities are as nice as any you'll find. The quality of racing has traditionally been lower than in neighboring Maryland, which means that it provides an excellent proving ground for new horsemen. What's more, the old snobbism of Maryland trainers hesitant to ship "over the mountain" is slowly subsiding. Purses are gaining weight, and winning there is not as easy as it looks.

Pennsylvania racetracks do the job, however blandly. Pennsylvanians are basically nice people. They are also tough, especially when it comes to winter night racing memorable for a piercing wind which needles through fabric, fur and skin.

The big operations are Penn National and Keystone. These tracks are fair, the management decent and the clientele by and large blue collar. It's good meat and potatoes racing.

Summertime resort tracks dot the coast replete with flowers and sometimes a refreshing breath of sea air. Delaware Park was known for years as the Saratoga of the South with its beautifully structured layout, its meadows and shady trees. Another standout, Monmouth Park in **New Jersey**, is as strikingly neat and clean as a military base. Holiday-close to New York, its purses are big and the whole operation is first class.

New Jersey's Meadowlands stands as a monument to human ingenuity: it was dredged out of swampland. Horsemen used to hustle from all over to ship horses in because Meadowlands-based horses were thought to be chronically plagued with soot and lung ailments. While this is no longer the case, shipping there can still be worthwhile if only to wander through the 25th century module situated atop the grandstand. Cloistered in casino-like elegance, bar flies and diners can squint at races broadcast on Star Trek banks of TV sets which are adjusted to whatever tint suits them best. Even Buck Rogers would be impressed.

Up North. The **New York** Racing Association (NYRA) is aristocracy. Belmont and Aqueduct will overwhelm you while you stargaze at the horse heroes of the day. Make the journey upstate to Saratoga in early August before the grounds have been trampled by invading fans. Saratoga is memories of sunlight filtering through the tall backstretch trees, of watching phantom horses gallop in the early morning haze while you enjoy a trackside breakfast of succulent Hand melon.

Some say great things about **New England** racing, especially those who have shipped up fit horses well before the local boys have had a chance to stretch their limbs in the first spring thaw. There is nothing that can ever compare with a legal scam!

Across the Land. Trumpets herald bettors throughout the states. While Kentucky with its blue grass and its Derby is part of American folklore, few outsiders know much about racing in hinterland states like South Dakota and Idaho. But racing's popularity in every corner of North America is indisputable: over 75 million fans swing the turnstiles annually. The lion's share—some 50 million of them—have been heading into Thoroughbred tracks.

Arlington Park (Illinois), Oaklawn Park (Arkansas) and Ak-Sar-Ben (Nebraska) are some of the big-name Mid-western tracks. Yet it has taken an upstart like California to rival New York's century-long aura with dazzling tracks, purses, trainers and horses. The East Coast-West Coast rivalry hovers at a stand-off: few runners have risen whose talents can bridge fast-track California and the weightier strips back East.

Parimutuel lobbying efforts have been building up steam in non-racing states specifically to counter the objections of conservative church groups and humane societies. Recently, there seem to have been as many failures as successes: the biggest setback came in Texas; the flashiest success story belongs to Oklahoma. But this is one issue that will never say die. Wherever people love horses and states love tax dollars, there will eventually be racing.

The truth of the matter is that any racetrack is a horseman's Valhalla. It is here that all the planning, spending and dreaming come to hand. You'll feel instantly at home. The steepest requirement for good memories and total enjoyment is that your horses run well and win.

BULLY BOY

Special Size won at every track from Belmont to bush league. Sprinter or stayer, he could handle anything from four furlongs on up to a mile and an eighth. On dirt, turf or tarmac road.

The horse was built like a fullback, with a mentality to match. Racing was just an excuse to hammer the competition face down into the ground.

Running low on his luck when we came along, x-rays showed that Size had been working with four broken bones. Kept right on roaring through the stretch like a battle-scarred tank, gun turret blazing and jock clinging to his mane for life.

Might have lost a step or two since his Super Bowl days, but this warhorse was still your best bet in any photofinish play. Special Size had a nose for the wire.

☊ Chapter Two ☊

ORGANIZATION

ANY TIME, ANY PLACE, ANY SPRAY

Tuffy Hacker earned his name. Nobody ever called him Beverly P. Hacker and lived. There are different ways of being tough, and he passed every test.

Entered a little filly in an $11,500 claiming contest for three-year-old maidens. Everybody knew that this trainer won one out of every three starts, so any starter of his was worth a second glance. We reached for a claim slip and filled it out . . . just in case.

Like all first-time starters, there wasn't much to go on. Any Spray looked like a rat. We crumbled the claim slip and walked away.

Too slight, too plain. All she could do was run, and run she did. Two months after the claim slip lay plucked by the seagulls in the county dump, Any Spray had won five in a row capped by a stellar performance in a high class stake.

Tuffy took a chance and let his filly get her feet wet—learn to win—on an easy level. He won big. We played it safe and lost out on one of the best fillies of her generation.

Be smart. Don't call this man Bev.

RACING STABLES

The papers are filled with the glory of stakes horses and the superstars of the racing scene. But most of us have no idea how to make the transition from our own unheralded ambitions to these widely publicized levels of racing brilliance. Racing has few manuals for success; it's too unpredictable for money-back guarantees. Yet the more you know about racing, the easier it will be for you to build up a creditable racing stable.

Racing is expensive. And hand-in-hand with money, it requires touch and insight. What we are addressing here is not how much money you spend, so much as how to get a good rate of return on your dollars, particularly in terms of pleasure and acclaim. That means winning. Bigger and better purses with evermore talented horses. But don't let yourself forget that, more than anything else, racehorses will demand endless reserves of patience. They need to be given time to develop, rest between races, and recover from troubles of every degree.

There have always been brave men who have set out to create the ideal horse operation practically overnight with huge outlays of cash. In times of economic uncertainty, though, most investors aren't as willing to pour millions into something as exotic as racehorses. If you are in a cautious mood you may even want to start out on the least expensive level, but it still doesn't mean that you won't be able to build your operation into a first class outfit. You can invest any amount, profit from and enjoy racing as long as you know what you're getting into. Hopefully the money you spend will be free and unencumbered, your conscience at ease. Too much pressure to win and meet bills can rob the pleasure from any sport. Horses are not highly liquid assets.

The Plan

By investing the best part of your bankroll in immediately useful horseflesh, you can easily lay the working foundations for building a sizeable and profitable stable. Your stable's money will go further if you initially steer clear of the bigger tracks. You'll have a better shot at those sweet purses after you've built up your expertise and subsequently your stock.

For a stable that will be diversified and soundly grounded, plan on claiming (buying directly from races) 60% of your overall livestock needs, while buying privately or at auctions another 20% and breeding the remaining 20%. Smart management shows that a strong core of veteran claiming level horses with proven, if limited, ability can generate a good day-to-day cash flow. This can be used to underwrite the training bills of more expensive or promising stock that needs an extra amount of pampering to reach its potential. Cash flow is the key.

The essential idea is to try to make your operation self-supporting from the very start. Whatever is spun off in the way of profits can be used to upgrade your stock. In theory it is only a matter of time before your stable becomes a powerhouse and you hit the jackpot with a big horse.

This format goes directly against every fledgling owner's desire to be immediately and exclusively associated with horses of the finest feather. The sooner you can disabuse yourself of this snobbism, the more rewarding racing will become. Rumor has it that a well-heeled stable once spent a million bucks before it won a race. Is that fun? Choose your weapons.

Any balanced approach is better than putting all your money into a single expensive racehorse, toying with swift disaster. It's too easy to lose everything and learn nothing in return. With all your hopes and aspirations centered on one animal, chances are that your judgment will be demolished both by your eagerness to race and your fear of losing your one and only racehorse in a claiming level contest. Frustration abounds. Running a horse when he's not ready or at an exalted level means facing defeat time and again, which is demoralizing for everyone, horse included.

As soon as you have received your basic racing education and have earned a degree of solvency, you'll be ready to shift the emphasis of your racing stable to equal parts claiming, buying and breeding. Like any good system, your racing stable should evolve with your expertise and financial strength. It is expected to grow and field better horses.

Owning racehorses reeks of glamor, but that's only to tourists living outside the sport. Horses teach you humility. It's not unusual, although ironic, to get a magazine featuring a star of the moment who died or fell from the heavens before the print was dry. That racing glory is elusive and ephemeral makes it all the sweeter, and reason enough to learn the tricks of staying in the game. There are some days that success can only be measured in terms of staying alive.

CHARLICO

Interested in seeing your horses race all week long? Then get your feet wet at a little track. Be a big frog in a little pond. You can have twice the fun at half the cost.

You'd do well to start out with a stable of four horses at the nearest half-mile track and—if you must—a couple of horses at a mile track, the local big-time. Or any practical variation on this theme. Six horses can give you good racing even though about a third are bound to be on the sick, injured or green list at any one time.

Farm Club

The value of a small track like Charles Town, West Virginia is heavily weighed in terms of education and entertainment. You don't get rich, but you do learn. It's a great kindergarten. The costs of making mistakes and gaining experience don't go sky-high.

The country pace can be a pleasant tonic for horse and human. Sort of a health spa for horses who need a holiday from a tough campaign and for those who are literally on their last legs. Owners get a break with the night racing set-up, which gives them time to relax and enjoy racing outside of the workday hours.

Major League

With two horses at Pimlico (or at a similar mile track in any racing state), you can maintain a presence in the land of lucrative races. The top non-stakes money is double West Virginia's purses. Maryland mile tracks are tough and prestigious.

Still, it pays to remember that Maryland-class horses don't come cheap. If you get a dud it will cost you plenty, while a bad investment at a small track can be written off as petty cash. So decide fast if a horse is really Maryland material. The meter is ticking away at premium per diem, twice the country rate.

If you have confidence in yourself and are willing to learn, it won't be long before you can build a force at any track. But first, practice your poker where the stakes are small.

Racing Divisions

The beauty of a league system is that you can conveniently shift stock back and forth, provided that you make your intentions clear from the start to both trainers. Go ahead and push lackluster stock off the expensive circuit and down to the small track, where it can shine. No point in keeping cheap horses at steep prices. Then you can easily move promising horses up from the minors to let talent compete for a fancy purse.

Having two—or more—complementary divisions presupposes a good working relationship between the trainers. Since most trainers equate the number of horses under their shedrow with dollar signs of success, they will often fight tooth and nail to hang onto blatantly unsuitable stock. If two trainers are constantly at each other's throats with bitter words of jealousy and disapproval, cooperation is doomed.

With astute management, you should eventually find that you have acquired more and more mile track horses and perhaps a star or two who could compete at any top level track. Racing divisions are not immortal. They are a system which reflects your needs of the moment. When you are ready to take on different fields of conquest, set up more racing divisions at other tracks.

You should never feel that you're slumming by initially keeping the preponderance of your racing stable at a small track. These tracks can win your heart by their very lack of snob appeal. Racing is all. Fans will drive all the way out there from the cities because they can't get enough of the sport, but those who only wish to see and be seen may stay away in droves. Racing is real, not just a frivolity that you can pick up and put down. It draws you into its world and tests your genuineness of spirit.

Financial Reality

The costs of racing are staggering. It's not unusual to spend more for a horse than what most people live on. The only way to rationalize these costs is to remind yourself that racehorses have earning power. Treat the venture as a business investment. You are ploughing in money with the expectation of getting it back and more. No need to feel guilty: you'll be aiding the economy and putting people to work.

Make your way slowly into racing. Accumulate horses in pace with your know-how. You must realize from the outset that start-up expenses and frustrations are bound to be high. Only with shrewdness and luck can racing pay for itself.

Success can be nickel and dime or it can come big. Hawksworth Farm found the pot of gold at the end of the rainbow when it syndicated Spectacular Bid for $22 million, up considerably from his original purchase price of $37,000. Hawksworth's owner, the savvy Harry Meyerhoff, had ironically chosen black and blue silks to remind himself of the financial drubbing dealt to owners. Some say he still insists that the bargain price of Spectacular Bid should be computed at $2 million, the amount Harry spent for not-so-good horseflesh before capturing the Bid.

Records. Keep good records of whatever you spend in racing, because tax regulations can be coaxed into giving horsemen a much-needed break. Incorporating your stable will help establish that it's a bona fide business and not a hobby. A hybrid corporate structure called Sub-chapter S is popular because it allows any losses to be written off on your personal tax bill, while limiting liability to the racing company. You will still be expected to turn an appreciable profit at least two out of seven years. (See Chapter Seven.)

Meticulous records will also help you pinpoint the expenses and earnings of each racehorse to show which ones are and are not paying their way. The cost of daily subsistence takes in far more than the board bill per diem. Don't forget medical expenses, which can be substantial even for healthy horses that only need vitamins, electrolytes and so forth. Then there are bills for shoeing, dentistry, vanning, tips for grooms, restaurant checks on racing days . . . an endless array of expenses which add up but can easily be covered by a winning horse.

Perspective. Maintaining your financial sanity is hard in the never, never land of racing. There are so few ways to measure what you get against what you spend other than with the finality of the bottom line. But plenty of sharp operators figure that for anyone who owns racehorses, money can't mean a thing.

This is not a country club. Don't let horsemen play one-upmanship with you. Get your money's worth; stop worrying about looking cheap. What you think of other people should count for more than what they think of you.

The incidence of quick in-and-out investors shows that financial debacle and ego pulverization take a bloody toll in racehorse owners. The byword is that 90% of all owners lose money. To stay in for the long and hopefully fruitful haul, it helps to have spirit of adventure and be slightly masochistic. Any die-hard horseman can be counted on to put any racing profits right back into his stable.

TRAINERS

Newcomers need a guardian angel to escort them safely into the racing world. Asking friends for advice is dicey. They can become treacherous creatures who end up selling you stock and schemes you wouldn't touch without your innocence.

Some new horsemen will actually enjoy racing in partnerships and syndicates as a way of spreading the risk while learning the game, but like carpooling, this approach has limited appeal—racehorse ownership is almost too personal to share.

©DAILY RACING FORM

'IT'S SAFE TO SAY I'M SPEAKING FOR ALL THE SYNDICATE MEMBERS WHEN I SAY THAT YOU GAVE THAT HORSE A LOUSY RIDE.'

For those who plan to go it alone in a big way, there are fine bloodstock agencies and stable agents offering knowledgeable, disinterested advice for a hefty fee. Otherwise, the burden rests squarely on your trainer to become your guide, confidant, mentor and key to the success of your racing stable.

Who

It's important to do some reflecting before choosing a trainer so that you can come to terms with what your needs and preferences are. Make sure from the start that you can live with a trainer's personality, horsemanship and organization. Changing trainers later on can be as traumatic and messy as a divorce in the close-knit racetrack community. Owners with their largely absentee status are often considered meddlesome boobs who have too much money for their own good. They are easily cast as the offending party.

Since your trainer will be your single most important contact with the racetrack, good vibes and good communication with him will be the basis of your confidence in this business venture. The ideal trainer is sensitive, intelligent and aggressive. You'll want your trainer to appreciate your interest in racing and understanding of the sport. To that end, he should be able to level with you comfortably on a one-to-one basis. Don't put up with the pompous posturing of an all-knowing hardboot. Go with a contemporary you can talk to.

There is something to be said for hiring a trainer who is in with the in-crowd. Clout counts, especially when it comes to getting good jockeys, stall space and favors here and there. Maryland tracks in particular used to cater to very large claiming-oriented stables in a mutually beneficial way. In return for allotting certain trainers a virtually unlimited amount of stall space (though not always at the track in session), management was assured of a huge and ready pool of useful runners. Most other racing locales set ironclad limits.

But even though the trainers of these giant Maryland-based operations tend to rank high in the national standings, new owners would probably prefer to get more personal attention and see a less ruthless approach to the claiming game. The best idea is to pick a trainer just below the top and possibly one who owns a few racehorses so that he will empathize with an owner's position. On a precautionary note, find a trainer who makes his living through purse winnings and not through betting.

Set up interviews with a prospective trainer just as you would check out any new employee. Be sure to discuss if he can accept the degree that you want to become involved in running your racing stable. Trainer/owner relationships call for reciprocal sensitivity even in ridiculously small considerations. For example, common decency tells you not to phone your trainer past his nine o'clock bedtime, just as you wouldn't appreciate a ring at five o'clock in the morning when his day begins.

A good trainer's organization is integral to his success. The racing world has traditionally been dominated by colorful personalities and a rigid caste system, with trainers reigning as the kingpins. The crews of exercise boys, pony riders, grooms and hotwalkers seem to be a mixture of dedicated horsemen and derelicts who don't object to the low pay and awkward hours. These positions are now frequently used as stepping stones for upwardly mobile help en route to becoming trainers or jockeys.

A Little Respect

Mutual respect will be enhanced between you and your training outfit if you take pains not to sound like an ignoramus. Here, long-time horseplayers take the edge by having track ritual and the language virtually in their bloodstreams. Unfortunately, a horseplayer's skill can suffer in the transition from bettor to owner. Betting instincts easily become clouded by knowing so many more variables about a horse's condition than those presented in the cold, hard statistics of the trackman's bible, the *DAILY RACING FORM*.

In the quest for understanding, racing can be as much of a commitment as your time and resources will allow. Read everything in print, which will mean keeping up with hundreds of periodicals. No one can do without the *DAILY RACING FORM* and two special weeklies, *THE BLOOD-HORSE* and *THE THOROUGHBRED RECORD*, which are both published in Lexington, Kentucky. You should also talk at length with other horsemen and watch all the racing you can. Each race you see will make it easier to spot problems you might be able to avoid to make your own horses win.

Race-watching is a pleasant duty which makes it easy to gain the support of others who must live with your enthusiasms. Racetrack amenities help. The nationwide catering service of Harry M. Stevens has elevated trackside dining to levels unattainable at the most fashionable tracks in France and England. Some track restaurants even furnish TV sets at each table which can be switched off the inhouse circuit and tuned in to cartoons and football games for the truly bored.

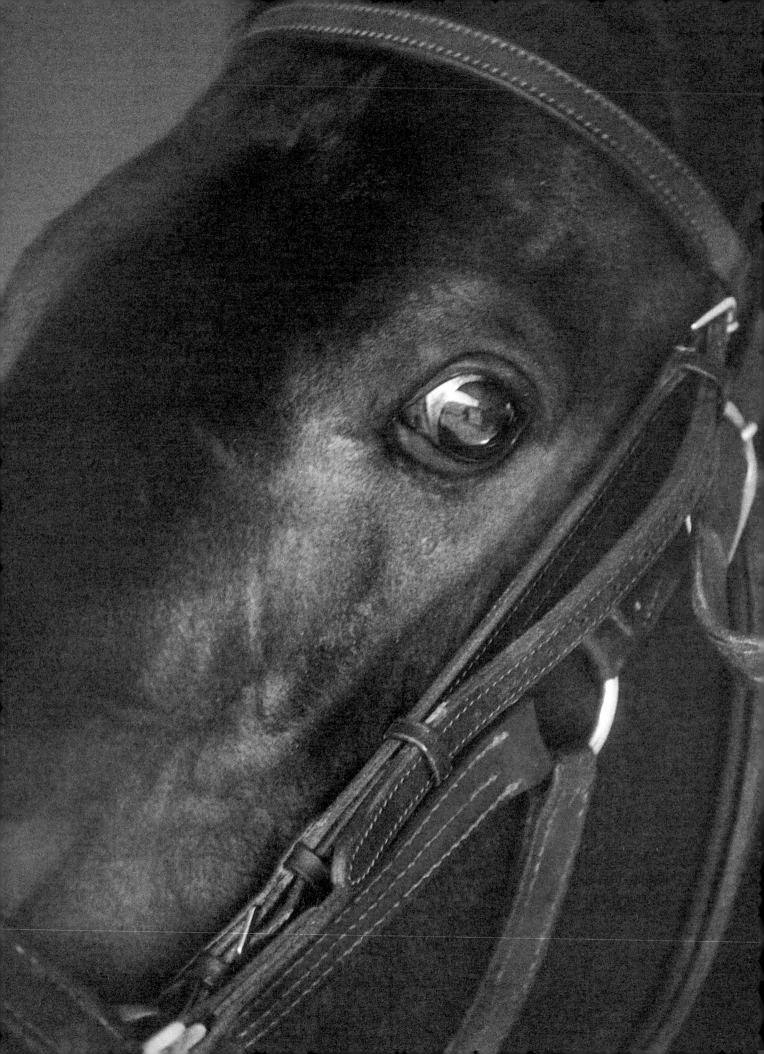

LIFERS

Mile Track

Maryland's Scott Regan is a rugged Irishman and a businessman par excellence, who combines acumen with ambition in a winning way. His organization is awesome. All-pro. He belongs on the list of leading trainers.

Scott is forthright. Always has the guts to tell it like it is. The truth can hurt, but it usually saves an owner money in the long run. When you get to this point, the trainer is your friend and comrade-in-arms.

Danny Davis is Scotty's right-hand man. The kind you'd like to send out to fight your wars for you. He is competitive and violently loyal. As fierce as a Gurkha warrior.

Danny grew up on the track. An intuitive horseman with inbred knowledge, he'll do anything for his horses. Work all day and all night. When they win, you know it's worth it.

Half-Miler

Lee Couchenour is the priest. Racing is his vocation. Helpers are good, but nobody works as hard as he. All his horses get a full measure of personal attention and affection. They grow fat and sassy. Impeccably groomed, they're the class act of the track.

The world is discovering Lee. His barn overflows with both promise and the last dregs of hope. Abandoned cats have always found a home. Now there's a contingent of castoff horses from Lee's buddies on the Maryland circuit. If anybody can turn them around, you know Lee can.

Lee is good to his owners, too. He will discuss their horses with genuine interest. He is a scholar in the world of horses, backed up with a computer-like mind. Never condescending, always patient, Lee's life is racing and it's almost heaven . . . in West Virginia.

But just beyond the Shenandoah shine the lights of New York. You'll find him there someday, still rubbing his own horses. Some things like pride you never outgrow.

STOCK

Let's assume that you choose your trainer first and set out with him to accumulate the best stock for your stable. (See Chapter Five.)In choosing your workaday horses, keep in mind the year's racing schedule so that you can pick stock whose running style will be right in tune with ongoing and upcoming track meets.

Most states, like Maryland, apportion racing days among their racecourses so that these tracks never have to compete against each other for the racing dollar. Consolidation is in the cards, though, and one or more Maryland tracks is slated for oblivion, the outback status of a training track. Racing should improve there with the best facilities gaining additional days. And life should become simpler for those who follow racing's gypsy trail.

In the traditional picture, the four different Maryland tracks used to maintain distinctive personalities. Their idiosyncrasies may actually have grown less pronounced over the years, thanks to the exceptional care given to these racing strips.

Unfrozen Bowie was often notoriously heavy and slow-going, which favored closers who liked to lope along in back of the field and come from behind to win once the frontrunners had been worn out trying to explode through the muck. In contrast, Pimlico was once known as the perfect speedtrack—hard and fast—so that frontrunners could easily get loose and sail on home.

Timonium in August made good, old-fashioned fairground racing. A tiny five-eighths of a mile oval, its tight turns were ideal for horses with an early lick and for good curve runners.

Early on, Laurel earned industry praise for its extensive face-lifting program to develop a fair and safe course featuring races coming out of a well-designed "chute" or straightaway. Other Maryland tracks took the cue and also went in for a little nip and tuck to improve things all around.

For years, only Laurel and Pimlico have been able to offer turf races (on the grass) in Maryland. Even there, turf races are infrequently carded—never in winter weather—and are usually restricted to a higher calibre of horse because of the difficulty of turf upkeep. That's why a turf horse, unless he's outstanding, would be of limited use.

Staking a Claim

You're now ready to hunt for a few hard-knocking horses from claiming level races as the groundwork of your new racing stable. Look for horses with slightly diversified talents, track bias and running style aside. There is no point in stocking your stable with horses that all need to run on the same level and at the same distance. Having to stick more than one horse into a particular race is a real bore and a financial waste of time.

Once you have decided on the array of runners you need, the next step is to pour over the *DAILY RACING FORM's* past performance summaries on all the horses racing in each card. It may take days to spot a good claim. Or they may all come on the same racing card. Forestall the impulse to buy en masse. Limit your claims to one a day, even though the only legal restriction is one per race. Your selections need to be individual to be well-considered.

You'll recall that claiming races were talked about earlier as a clever device to ensure that all the horses in a particular race are well-matched by making each one carry a similar price tag. Most racehorses belong in claimers, and they range in the mid-Atlantic states from $2,000 to $35,000. Although claiming races rank in prestige below allowance and stakes races (which rely on specific conditions and weights to balance a race's outcome), claiming level horses can be solid, useful runners. In contrast to horses which you buy pre-racing age or you breed, they come with an established past performance record showing you what kind of talent and expertise you are getting. But you'll still have to keep your fingers crossed that any horse you claim will be sound enough to continue racing to form.

Claiming is no Aladdin's lamp. You'll find that out as soon as you claim an injury-ridden animal. If you're lucky, though, you might just pick up a very talented horse who, for correctable reasons, happens to be racing below his potential. The best claims can provide you with immediate racing pleasure, experience and monetary return.

There are innumerable and locally varying claiming rules designed to make horsemen think before they leap. The horse you claim is yours regardless of whether he does badly or dies during the race. You should expect to run a claimed horse at 25% more (usually the next price level) for 30 days from the date of claiming. It's the law. During the next couple of months you can't sell him and you can't even ship that horse out to run at another track until the meet ends. You're "in jail," so be sure the horse is worth it.

Every horseman has to learn to play a shell game with his own claiming level stock. The basic idea is to run a useful horse on as low a level as possible to take advantage of easier competition without making it too tempting for another horseman to claim him. On the other hand, it can be equally gratifying to beguile some fool into claiming a totally unsatisfactory horse from you. Or maybe he's not such a fool and will know a trick or two that's passed you by. He might just turn that horse around.

Most tracks require you to race a horse during their meet to become eligible to do any claiming. The traditional end-run around this dilemma is to enter a "policeman," which means that you finagle a deal to buy a horse from a friend or your trainer on a temporary basis for one dollar and run him in your name just to get qualified. An easier scam is to have an eligible friend claim the horse you want and then sell it to you privately after waiting the required months and a judicious timespell longer. Both practices are dubious but done.

Tears. All new owners need some heavy-duty counseling to prepare them for the terrifying prospect of having a horse claimed off them. Tantrums are routine. After stomping around in indignation, some owners will resort to sniveling revenge by making an ill-considered claim off the same fellow who took a horse from them. They might even want to reclaim their own horse. Dumb moves. When a horse is gone, he's gone. Fall in love with people, not investments.

FOOLS

Class can go to your head. Cephalonian had it. He was a hard-running horse with plenty of heart and a string of stake victories. But treachery lurked in the talent he showed: exceptional depth of chest and lungs overpowered legs of a lesser scope.

When Ceph first ran for a tag, we didn't think, we just grabbed. The track ambulance set him down in front of our barn with one ankle dragging along on the ground.

Two years went by of witchcraft and rest, so the track was buzzing when Cephie finally wound up for the test. Easy. Popped his head through the gate and sailed clear of the field. A prince among plodders. The way the horse'd won even under a hold made railbirds murmur about how high he might go.

So the good man Alfred kept Cephalonian rubbed to a sunset glow, and dug deep into his pocket for fleece-covered gear. Al even lined the stall shoulder-high with protective hay bales before each race. There was class in Alfred, too.

The day they claimed the big horse away, the shedrow grew cold. We went and claimed him back.

But the welcome was bittersweet as Cephalonian was once more chauffeured to the door, facing another year off with a chipped ankle bone. Alfred smiled. Cephie whinneyed. He was home again, this time to stay.

And we were a little bit broker.

A racing stable is like having a fleet of limousines. Every once in a while you need to trade up for new ones and cull out the old. Claiming does this naturally. You should only want to keep horses that you can move up into allowance or stakes company. Everything else is by nature for sale.

There is plenty of cold, hard cash to be made by coolly buying and selling racehorses through the claim box, particularly young stock. As you grow more sophisticated with the system, and more hard-nosed, you'll want to learn where claiming is the most feral. Then, if you have to raise money in a hurry, all you need do is ship a few horses to tracks where horsemen howl for new blood.

Once you've had a few horses claimed off you, you'll find it isn't so bad. Claiming may be the epitomy of all that's crass in racing, but it's a vital part of the game. Kiss them goodbye and wish them well.

Bidding for Greatness

Stock that you tend to get the most dangerously attached to is acquired through auctions as well as private sales and breeding. Its raceworthiness is neither as clearly defined nor as limited as stock that has been claimed. All you have to base your hopes and dreams on is conformation and pedigree.

There are Thoroughbred auctions scheduled throughout the year. Most focus on a particular age group of racing stock. You can purchase your prospective racehorse in utero along with the broodmare or as a weanling, yearling, or a two-year-old in training. There are a few horses of racing age offered at auctions, but they are usually too washed up to run.

Auction prices can be cheaper for younger horses, although you have to remember that the time, money and risk involved in bringing a horse to the races will add up so that your total outlay of cash could be more than if you had bought the horse at a later stage. Be sure to doublecheck the current tax provisions, especially the depreciation scales, and see how they relate to buying horses in the different age groups.

Also keep in mind that the younger your new horse is, the longer you'll have to wait before knowing the thrill of racing. But if you already have some ready-to-run claimers on the track, you won't begrudge the time and money it takes to develop potentially great stock.

Horsemen should go to as many auctions as possible to get a feel for the market, to know what is available and at what price. Window-shopping knowledge can be especially helpful when you need to negotiate a private sale.

Maryland auctions used to be considered bargain basement with the designer shows going on in Kentucky, New York and to some extent Florida. In the late seventies, prices got pretty healthy all over. With new tracks slated to open in the Mid-West, and old ones to reopen in the East, the domestic demand for good horseflesh should soar some more.

Astronomical profits made at the top sales were initially helped along by the depressed dollar and good performance abroad of American-breds, which brought out a flood of foreign investors. This was a dramatic reversal of the post-war trend of U.S. buyers scouring Europe to find dirt-cheap but classy bloodlines and bringing them home to roost.

Commercial breeders in this country picked up right away on the new international demand for U.S. horses and boosted prices even further by competing among themselves for the best breeding stock. Breeding top class animals for the selling ring became much more lucrative than breeding to race. A well-bred filly could now be worth her weight in gold as a broodmare even if she would never see the racetrack. On the other hand, sire prospects below the top level have always been relatively less valuable because they are less in demand. One stallion can service some 50 mares a year.

Preparation. Be professional, do some spadework long before the first horse is marched to the block. Both you and your trainer should take the time to pour over the sales catalog, which is usually available three to four weeks in advance by ordering it from the sales company or by picking it up in the Racing Secretary's Office at any nearby track. Draw up a budget of sorts and go over each interesting prospect on the sales grounds to look systematically for disabling conformation faults.

If you're out to spend millions, spend a few thousand first to get the horse "scoped," which is an internal inspection of the respiratory system, and x-rays, measurements and gait analysis movies made. Auction house warranties are extremely limited in length and coverage for eyes, bones, reproductive capacity and wind. Auctioneers should always volunteer the information that a horse "cribs" or gulps air.

While it ought to hold true that you could corner the market on good horses by spending endless amounts of money, one of racing's charms is that it is perversely democratic. A "by Truck out of Winchester" bumpkin might end up kicking sand in the face of your expensive and elegantly-bred acquisition. The often dismal race earnings of auction sale-toppers would indicate that nature is contrary enough to make scrappiness prevail at a disconcerting rate.

Breeding Blues

By keeping an eye on the sales catalogs and auction results, you'll have gotten some idea of the most fashionable pedigrees. But before working out any breeding arrangements for your broodmare stock, first take a look at the stud horses that interest you and see if they excite you in the flesh.

Granted that choosing the right stallion is fundamental, horsemen still put more faith in the "bottom line," that is, the quality of the broodmare and her family, as the dominant factor in producing a head-turning runner. Not only does she pass on the size of her heart in the strength of her genes, but she is responsible for the health of the embryo during gestation and imparts attitudes of aggression and command during the suckling stage. Studies show that each group of horses develops a graded social system of alphas, betas and bad news zedas, and that foals will generally assume the same pecking order as their mothers.

A springtime crop of foals is a heartwarming sight, but be forwarned that good broodmares can come high, and that stud fees and boarding bills mount up fast. The entire process of getting a homebred to the races takes over three years from conception and can be about as fast-paced and thrill-packed as watching the grass grow. And you might spend all that time and money just to find out you've got yourself a plater that someone else will claim from you as soon as he becomes useful.

Despite the drawbacks, enough horsemen keep a hand in breeding to allow the tracks to field full races. Once you have a system set up, and are not on pins and needles waiting for the first class to graduate into racing, it's intriguing to have a fresh supply of talent automatically coming up from the farm every year. Hopefully, the horses already on the track will be decent enough to pay the early bills for all these homebreds, the stuff of racing dreams. (See Chapter Three.)

In search of character—the indefinable edge . . .

BY JOVE

The name fit. Jove in Motion was a dappled gray vision that floated along, dragging his earthbound groom from shedrow to paddock.

Jove had one bad knee and two big ankles. No matter the pain, the horse was a pro.

His trainer tried to stand him for hours in buckets of ice to cool out those legs and lessen the strain. But at the sound of the bugle call before every race, Jove would rear from his tub in a one-horse hailstorm. Stamping ice cubes and kicking grooms, the old horse kept snorting, "Coach, send me in!"

There's one thing this horse will always win: your heart.

ALL JOIN HANDS

After you bring together a good training outfit with useful and diversified racing stock, there is still room and a continuing need for you to guide your racing stable. It's your money at stake! One way you can always help is to keep an eye on the condition books of area racetracks so that if your horses aren't being placed in races they can win, it won't be through oversight. Most horses race best at the track where they're stabled, but if a horse can't handle the course conditions, shipping out to another track is better than trailing the field at the wire, ignominiously called U.T. or "up the track."

A racehorse owner has to be a special breed of horseman. Despite the degree of control you can hold by intelligently monitoring your operation, there's not one of us who doesn't feel a sense of despair and helplessness when things go wrong. It helps to be a realist. Remember that typically 30% of your racehorses will not be race-worthy at any one time. Keep in mind that recovery periods from injury and illness can be twice as long as forecast, and that afterward most horses will need a few starts to find their stride again.

When physical problems first crop up, weigh a horse's talent against the expense of recovery and retraining—there is no guarantee that any horse will ever regain his form. Try to evaluate bad news objectively by reading up on the subject. Talk to the vet and everyone else involved. Suggest getting a second medical opinion or using an alternate treatment, perhaps one of the new Sportsmedicine approaches edging over the horizon. Be a regular pain in the ass. Training rules aren't engraved in stone.

Set-backs are endemic in this sport because Thoroughbreds are a particularly nervous breed and a few seconds of carelessness or bad luck can demolish your hopes and your investment. Since there are easier ways to lose a buck than with a ho-hum stable, you should try to limit your entourage to those creatures you have a genuine feeling for. You can always solicit and listen to advice, but only claim, bid on or breed horses that excite your imagination. You'll find that any mistakes you yourself make will be easier to live with than the mistakes of others.

Once you've taken the plunge of becoming an owner, greater understanding of the sport will be absorbed by osmosis over time. Racing is a life-long love.

○ Chapter Three ○

LIFESPAN

'MAKE UP YOUR MIND: IT'S HER OR ME!'

BREEDING

The overall quality of U.S. racehorses should take a giant leap forward as the commercial breeders, spurred on by a champagne market around 1980, have jumped into the fray in a big way. The haphazard breeding of any old broken-down race mare to a kind of nice stallion became strictly backyard stuff. Mares with good pedigrees were dredged up and dusted off, while the line for the most fashionable stallions stretched around the block.

While taking a good look at breeding can fill in your understanding of how a racehorse is developed, any new owner should be talked out of diving head-long into an extensive and expensive breeding scheme. Rocks abound. It is a long-term and often frustrating investment, especially if you don't know exactly what you're aiming for. You could end up with a barnful of misfits.

Outfits set up primarily as racing stables have a way of backing into breeding. A decent filly gets too sore to run and—presto!—you have a brand-new brood-mare. But no matter how great a racehorse sire you may have lined up for her, don't kid yourself that you have found a particularly cheap way to get your hands on good stock. You've got stud fees, years of farm per diem and big training bills to look forward to before any homebred is ready to race. You may even want to go out and buy a farm just so that you can pet some noses while paying the bills. This is a natural progression.

Unless you've bought yourself a fancy broodmare with a star-studded produce record, you're going to have to wait three to four years before knowing if your mare was worth breeding at all. In the meantime, you'll have welcomed two more foals on the ground from that same mare if you adhere to the common practice of breeding her back each year. Statistically speaking, the best racehorses should come from her second through fifth crops, although they could easily all be dogs.

You can always sell off accumulated offspring as pleasure horses if the brood shows no propensity for greatness. The key to remember is that it is easy to forgive and forget lousy horses, even homebreds. They don't hang around the house, smoke pot, borrow your car or come back to haunt you with grandchildren. If horses are no good, they go. They're a business, not a family.

Ways & Means

Techniques. Thoroughbred breeding has restraints imposed on it by the Jockey Club for better control and exclusivity. For example, the everyday technique of artificial insemination (AI) which is used with increasing frequency in livestock and humans is resolutely disallowed. (Don't even mention embryo transplants!) Flat racing's sister sport, harness racing, has encouraged AI for years so that a Standardbred sire can regularly service mares by the trackload with the help of semen extenders. In contrast, even the strongest Thoroughbred stallions working alone shouldn't handle many more than 50 mares per year. No matter. Few but the most successful sires ever get near to a full book.

Surprisingly enough, nixing AI has made Thoroughbred breeding much more democratic. With AI, popular stallions could conceivably dominate so completely that they would make it tough for the other guys on the block to get a date. Everybody in racing believes in fairy tales, so you have got to give the two-bit sire a chance to throw his champion foal.

The owners of top Thoroughbred stallions aren't hurt financially by limiting service to the select court of mares that a stallion can physically handle. Tight supply and a healthy demand can push stud fees through the ceiling.

The reigning king for years was Northern Dancer, who was able to command an astronomical fee "up front" (before breeding) even without the standard live foal guarantee. Assuming that you could pay this fee from petty cash, there was still little chance your best-bred mare could get past the receptionist. Syndicate owners of popular stallions are inclined to hoard their season shares for their own mares with an eye on the sky-rocketing prices paid for blue-blooded offspring.

When you have a new stallion, there's nothing like garnering some high auction prices for his progeny to set off a stampede of mares to his court. Prices are sometimes based on whim—two bidders fighting over a good-looking yearling—or on more salient factors like a stakes winner or two in a recent foal crop. But the very best assurance of a glowing auction price is a gilt-edged mare. The strength of her X chromosomes can determine heart size, and winning her big heart can make any stallion fashionable.

'I DON'T CARE IF YOUR NAME IS BOLD SO AND SO OR NATIVE SOMETHIN'... GET LOST!'

Age Groups. For clarity's sake, all Thoroughbreds celebrate birthdays on January 1 regardless of their actual date of birth. It's easy to see why uniformity is necessary: race conditions generally specify the age of the horses as a way of evening up the competition. Two-year-olds are usually not as developed or as fast as three-year-olds, who in turn need similar protection from racing against the hard-knocking four-and-up veterans. Handicappers find that sound older horses have the edge almost every time.

The all-important auction schedules would also be thrown into confusion with deregularized birthdays since auctions tend to specialize in age groups of horses. The most prestigious auctions of all are the yearling sales held each summer in Kentucky. For these sales, consignors want to be able to turn out a large, well-developed individual born as soon after January 1 as possible.

High stakes make commercial breeders cut the timing close. The equine gestation period is 11 months, and breeders start queing up outside the breeding sheds early in February. Waiting just a couple of weeks longer might prevent the disaster of a premature December foal that would be officially designated a yearling before it's a month old. Baksheesh will be called for to trigger a wave of yuletide amnesia among the barn help.

Farms generally separate male and female foals right from the start to prevent a preteen pregnancy. Puberty is thought of as 15 months, but this figure could be off by six months. At any rate, the boys do play rougher than the girls—rearing up on their hind legs and tearing off halterplates. Little Lord Fauntroy types, those million dollar sales prospects, are separated from everybody, period.

Male Thoroughbreds up to the age of five are called "colts" and the older ones are "horses." Along the same lines, young female horses are "fillies" and those above age five are "mares." Castrated males of any age are known as "geldings." Most trainers stand behind the popular view of gelding all male horses unless they are impressively bred. This is supported by chatter about how a horse's testicles might interfere with his leg action and how a gelding is supposed to be more tractable and single-minded about racing. Ironically enough, owners often end up paying about $50 a month in substitute male hormone shots for geldings and female horses to build up better muscle and provide a stallion's drive. Gelding racing stock barely figures unless a horse is dangerously fractious.

With few exceptions, horses must be gelded if they want to make a career switch to pleasure horse status. But be forewarned that former racehorses can make lousy riding horses. They have always been exhorted to run! Even if you get them to slow down, they're still likely to succumb to old racing injuries while pursuing the equal rigors of hunting and jumping.

NIGHTMARE

Varna II won them all—lots of stakes and lots of hearts. Bred to the greatest stallions of her generation, she gave the racing world stakes winners and stakes-winning grandchildren. Her pedigree was embossed in black type, the kind used to highlight the best horses.

She came to us as a 20-year-old castoff from a fancy breeding farm after they'd taken all that they could from her in the way of babies and tax write-offs. We shined her up and made her happy. But after 14 children, she deserved a rest. Her body rejected sperm, resorbed eggs, reinfected regularly.

Infections in broodmares are no small thing. If the immune system is weak, they can drag on for years and damage the tissue so badly that nothing helps. After months at a renowned broodmare hospital, she came home barren and we called it quits.

Save your money, be humane. Horses—even broodmares—are not machines.

*An asterisk before a name is the traditional way to denote a foreign-bred animal. The latest fashion is to show the country of birth in parentheses following the name.

Lights! Action! Two of the worst natural breeding months for horses are February and March, which are invariably busy times at Thoroughbred breeding farms. Mares can be tricked into ovulating early by lighting the barn mid-winter so their systems think that the long days of spring and summer are at hand. Lighting the barn for 16 hours a day for 60 days will stimulate the hypothalamus and coax a mare out of her winter anestrus. (Research promises to trim these hours and the resulting electric bills.) During the rest of the year, mares enter a period of estrus—"coming in season"—about every three weeks when they produce a follicle on the ovary which breaks off to become an egg. "Breeding on the follicle" is the optimal time just as in human fertilization.

Racemares may need a few months to be "brought down" before breeding. Time off helps cleanse out racing medication and male hormones. Some do fine straight from the track; others enjoy racing pregnant.

Each breeding farm vet has a roomy bag of tricks at his disposal. For example, he can encourage ovulation with hormones like prostaglandin if there's a problem with a non-cycling mare. Normally, though, the vet can rely on cycle guidelines handed to him by the farm manager and the teaser stallion: whenever a mare shows interest in the highly frustrated teaser stud, it's a good indication she's coming in heat. The vet can then "palpate" (feel the internal organs) to pinpoint the very best time for breeding. All this saves the stallion from being over-used. Just one cover at the right time can do the job.

Vets can also determine early in the game if a mare is in foal by using rectal palpation or the new ultrasound technology. Ultrasound is particularly valuable for detecting twins within 30 days. One of the embryos can then be pinched off or the whole thing aborted because twins are generally considered too weak to race.

Some broodmares, especially older ones, need to have their wombs sutured closed by the vet after breeding to keep out bacteria living in the air and in her urine and feces. This is called the Caslick procedure and the trick is to remember to snip the stitches when it is time for the mare to foal. When you see fillies and mares on the track with their rear ends taped shut, that's to prevent them from sucking wind. It looks silly and doubtfully scientific.

If springtime gives your mare a headache, you might be able to persuade a smaller breeding outfit to extend the breeding season beyond the June 30 date when most stud farms slam the shed doors shut. Old or ill mares who do not easily conceive can then be given a second chance at a perfectly natural summer breeding time, provided it doesn't get too damn hot. Overall, it makes good sense to elongate the breeding season so that there is less seasonal pressure on the stallion and the farm operation as a whole.

The biggest drawback to breeding late is that the resulting foal would be born at an unusually late date the following year. Commercial breeders could hardly be expected to go for this approach since they need early foals to shape into well-developed individuals by auction time. But those who breed their own racing stock should seriously consider the option of summer breeding. Many horses are not pushed to race as two-year-olds, and by the time they reach the three-year-old level, being a couple of months younger than their competition doesn't make that much difference.

Something else to think about if you are faced with the boring and expensive prospect of carrying empty broodmares into the next breeding year is finding an accommodating farm which will not only breed through the summer, but be willing to try some sort of pasture breeding. The original concept of throwing a stallion in with a bunch of broodmares and letting nature take its course can be pretty hard on the stallion and on mares that can't fend well for themselves. An intelligent modification being toyed with called "paddock breeding" puts only those mares in estrus out with the stallion. All the animals are taken in daily to be cleaned, fed and examined.

Even with the degree of control that paddock breeding affords, it goes without saying that few people would ever be willing to give expensive breeding stock that much freedom. In the traditional hand breeding method, each mare is cleaned and led to an equally sanitized stallion, and the animals are kept under strict control at all times. The romance may be gone, but the pheromones (sex smells) linger on.

While a stallion's world is largely feast or famine, the proper broodmare is pregnant year after year. Maximum resourcefulness has a broodmare foaling after 340 days and then being rebred on her foal heat, which occurs about a week after foaling. If she conceives again, she's all set to go home with suckling foal at her side and a baby in utero. The mare's body becomes so attuned to motherhood that it seems easier to keep a mare pregnant this way than it is to impregnate a barren or maiden mare. Nobody asks her what she thinks.

Farms. Choreograph your operation so that your mare will be sent to the breeding farm standing the stallion of your choice about a month before she is due to foal, which will give her plenty of time to get acclimated. Let the farm take care of everything, bill you and send her home after she has been declared in foal. You could even leave her there year-round, but the per diem would be hefty.

Some breeders take cost-cutting a step too far by trying to rush a home-based mare over to the stallion on breeding days only. This method requires an astute eye and often the help of a teaser stud to pinpoint when a mare is coming into heat. He'd bring on the common signs of estrus which are squatting, backing up to a horse, "winking" with the vagina and secreting a clear mucous. If she plainly "shows," there is still no guarantee you can get to the stud of your choice on D-day, since covers per day are limited for the health of the stallion. Farm-stationed mares are naturally given preference. By opting to pay the higher board per diem at the stallion's home farm for the duration of the breeding season, you can forego this hassle.

Foaling. Foaling in mares is as straightforward a process as it is in any other warm-blooded animal. Somebody with experience should still be on hand in case of complications, and it means a springtime of sleeplessness on breeding farms. Most of the trouble occurs when foals are presented skew-wise. Time is short, a half hour at most, and mares often die without some knowing and strong-armed help. You'll be spared great dark circles under your eyes if your mare is sent off to foal at the farm standing the prospective stud. Even so, if you care about her, you'll still want to know what she's going through.

Impending foaling is heralded by signs of "bagging up" for a couple of weeks and by colostrum dripping from the teats for a couple of days. When her time is close, the mare will get restless, then finally lie down and strain with contractions. In the right presentation, the foal's front feet come out first with his nose lying on top of the out-stretched legs. Everything else should slide out easily with the placenta breaking open naturally. The after-birth will be passed out in a few minutes time and the whole thing ought to be pieced together to make sure nothing remains inside the womb that could get infected. After resting a few minutes with death-like stillness, the mare will presently start licking her foal and he will begin his valiant struggle to stand and eventually nurse.

The umbilical cord stub should be disinfected right away with iodine and will later drop off. As a final touch, the foal is given an enema to help remove the meconium plug. Some farms will also zap a foal with a shot of antibiotics and tetanus, but this is optional. A niggling thought is that early shots might wreck the natural immunity a foal gets from his mother.

Your mare and her foal can be sent back to you as soon as she tests out pregnant, which can be ascertained fairly soon after she's been bred, thanks to sophisticated vet work. New foals on the farm are no trouble. If your mare trusts you, she'll let you pet her baby right away. Some foals become so confident and relaxed with the human touch that they will pop out of the stalls by themselves to frolic with the grooms.

Stud Power. Playing marriage broker to your mare isn't easy. Thoroughbred magazines regularly publish Stallion Registers early in the new year, but you'll want to have your mind made up long before then. Ads, word of mouth, pedigree, visual impact and sentimental attachment all go into the decision-making hopper.

The oracle of the breeding shed is Italy's Federico Tesio who bred the great Nearco and *Ribot. From schools of learned voyeurs comes a legacy of finely reasoned catch-words. Applying the terms "dosage," "chef-de-race," "nicks" and "outcrosses" has managed to befuddle breeders for years. Many will now admit that they are frankly more concerned with breeding what sells best. This means gambling on what will be fashionable, what the big buyers will be looking for, two years down the line. Even a computer isn't foolproof here.

A relatively new theory that departs from the "breed the best to the best and hope for the best" theory involves the idea of breeding physical balance into a racehorse. While most horsemen will cast an eye over a horse and give an instant verdict about his balance and ability, the advocates of this new theory take no such chances with their predictions. Measurements are made of almost every angle in a horse's body, then the results are run through a computer to see how they stack up. Enough statistics have piled up to reinforce the notion that top stakes horses and successful sires score highly on engineering balance.

To insure that this excellence is passed along to progeny, the theory goes on to dictate that you must breed horses of similar physical structure to each other. This part is revolutionary. Most horsemen have looked for compensating virtues to create the perfect specimen and would be inclined to breed a mare that's a touch too small to a large, rangy fellow, and so on.

Adventuresome horsemen will particularly enjoy breeding to unproven stallions that have one outstanding characteristic: high speed. According to studies at Virginia Tech, speed is the one attribute that can be counted on to be inherited by some 30% of a stallion's "get." An explanation for this might be that part of speediness stems from having inherited a good percentage of fast twitch muscle fiber. To simplify the theory, every horse is endowed with both fast twitch and slow twitch muscle fiber in certain fixed proportions. The prevailing thought of the new Sportsmedicine approach is that you can build up endurance through training but that the fiber capacity for speed must be inborn. Horsemen may make mincemeat of this theory but don't let them downgrade the lure of "cheap speed."

THE EARLY YEARS

Weaning

Foals usually stay with their moms for four to five months, and by weaning time they are eating a little feed here and there. If a mare has blatantly undesirable characteristics—a retiring attitude or exceptional viciousness—that you do not want her foal to pick up, plan on weaning when her foal is as young as one month old. The trend toward early weaning has been reinforced by the independent attitude and shining health which often blossoms thereafter.

Since the nutritional value of a mare's milk drops off quickly, weaning a foal early on well-balanced baby food makes sense healthwise for the pup. The mare stands to gain as well because a robust suckling foal can be a great drain on her, especially if she is pregnant again. Studies show that milk production peaks at four to six weeks, but foals keep on demanding hearty meals to sustain growth at the rate of four pounds a day and a couple of inches a week. At 12 months, a horse has gained 80% of his adult size. By age three, he can drive, drink and vote.

Old-timers and the superstitious among us believe in consulting the moon sign calendar, still printed faithfully in each copy of THE BLOOD-HORSE, to figure out the least traumatic weaning date. (See Appendix.)Legend has it that weaning should take place when the sign is in the lower legs or feet. The rationale is that the moon affects various parts of the body as it changes stages. Weaning is supposed to go more smoothly if the moon's influence is focused farthest away from the most upsettable part of the horse's body, the head. Horsemen should take every edge.

Weaning has infinite variations, none of them perfect. Some farms will take out one mare a day until there are no more left in a field of weanlings. Nice idea, but it leaves the moon sign theory in tatters. Another trick is to walk the unsuspecting mares into a new field and whisk away all the foals before they turn around. The drawback to this method is that it presupposes that your babies are halter-broken and can be led. Whichever way you choose, the whinneying is bound to grow pitiful at weaning time. But it soon dries up, just like the mare's milk.

If you have only one barn, it's a good idea to leave the mares outside and out of sight for the next few days until memories dim, rather than gathering together the family around the barn dinner table. The mares should be given less feed at this time anyway because the niacin in grain stimulates milk production.

Once weaned, the foal starts being treated like an adult and given even more human contact. If you run a relatively small breeding operation, it's an easy thing to lead in all the horses on a daily basis to be groomed and checked over, fed and put to bed. When it gets hot and insect-ridden in the summer, horses can be let out overnight and brought into the cool barn during the day.

All of this handling is diametrically opposed to the philosophy of keeping young horses battling in a herd until they are ready to be broken. Whether this is just a labor-saving device or is actually intended to bring out the tough-guy, fighting instinct is hard to say. Man-shy horses can be hell to work with and can lessen their innate value by spending much of their energy later on in life fighting off human help. Surviving the rough and tumble of their untamed youths may make fighters out of horses, but it also stands to leave them with only a couple of sound legs to run on.

Breaking

The majority of homebreds enjoy a halcyon life of growing and playing during the year between weaning and breaking. In the commercial breeding world, though, this period is the critical time to prepare for the stylish summer yearling sales. Smaller commercial outfits might do well to hand over the cream of their crop to agents who make a good living out of professionally preening young horses into showcase perfection. Months of closely supervised diet, exercise and corrective hoof trimming can turn a nice individual into a millionaire's "must-have."

Serious schooling starts for most trackbound animals in August of their yearling year. Those who break the yearlings—teach them to be ridden—like to get hold of their pupils while the weather is still warm and the animals are in a relatively nonchalant mood. Horses are basically cold-weather animals and nothing electrifies them like the first crisp days of autumn.

The commonly ascribed-to methods of breaking yearlings are much subtler than the antics of the Wild West. The whole process takes place over six weeks of daily sessions. Every trainer has a special touch. Some start out working yearlings on the lunge line—a long shank devised so that the horse can be worked in a large circle around the trainer. They might use a girth-like surcingle to give a horse the feel of something around his back. Others like to "drive" yearlings, which actually means following along on foot and steering the animal with a harness and reins. The rest may say to hell with it, and slap on a bridle and saddle right away. Whatever works, goes. Well-handled yearlings can be amazingly docile about the whole business, particularly if they are taught "in company" with their cohorts. In almost no time, your crazies will be trotting around like regular riding school ponies.

Nobody can overdo thoughtful handling and good schooling. Young horses are willing enough pupils and they generally get sweeter as they mature. Old horses are like old dogs. They resist new tricks and remedial schoolwork. Ingrained fears and habits may need brain surgery to correct.

'IF HE FEELS GOOD, I FEEL GOOD!'

58

LAST IN CLASS

Jay was a model workaholic. His new farm with its big mortgage gave him a five-star incentive. Hungry enough to take on any piece of business that came his way, Jay never quite figured on Dr. Suess.

The horse was a reform school heavy, vicious and mean. Two men had already tried, and almost died, breaking the surly colt.

Jay had the master's touch. God knows the saddle irritated Suess. Jay made him eat and sleep in it for three days until the horse was ready to concede the round. Now Suess couldn't wait to toss the man in the next.

Jay was too smart to play fair. Tied on floppy sacks of straw and noisy buckets to the saddle, instead of himself. One helluva junkyard. Suess' ears burned with embarrassment and he tried hard to ignore the ignominious baggage.

One day the clanking stopped. Dr. Suess looked back in time to see old Jay ease up into the driver's seat.

Even bad dudes will bow to a worthy foe.

Training Wheels

Classes are over and school is dismissed well before the winter weather. Most year-lings are turned out to relax and grow until mid–March of their two-year-old year, although a handful of horsemen believe in going on with young horses and galloping them right through the winter. If you decide to force-bloom two-year-old racehorses, you can sometimes take advantage of the easier fields in the earliest two-year-old races, particularly those in Florida and Southern California. In other parts of the country, though, two-year-old races are fairly rare until summer and aren't carded with any great regularity until autumn.

"Two-Year-Olds in Training" sales in the temperate states also wait until later in the year, long after the famous Florida wintertime sales. A warning: don't take the name of the sale too seriously. It is a fallacy to think that you could buy a horse from this type of sale and stick him in a race the next day. The usual sales criteria specify that a horse must have been in training for just 60 days if broken as a yearling and for 90 days if broken later. This training might only consist of a brush-up course in schooling on the farm and a passing familiarization with the track. Add another two to six months of full-priced training bills and you'll have a more realistic idea of what is traditionally called for to get an animal racing fit.

"Two-Year-Olds in Training" sales still generate plenty of interest because you can actually get to see how a horse moves on the track. There is a massive session scheduled before each auction when the horses are individually timed either at a gallop or while being "breezed," that is, set down to go fast. This gives a talented horse without great breeding the chance to turn a fair penny with a rousing workout.

Getting a horse race-ready for the first time is always a snail-paced process. It has to be slow because horses are animals that thrive on routine to build up their confidence, competence and capabilities. Young horses are also prone to "buck shins" if pushed too fast. This is a commonplace, but painful, condition which halts all progress for a couple of weeks. The less severe cases involve inflammation of the cannon bone covering, while the more serious ones might show up as micro-fractures of the bone.

Before a young horse can finally start in a race it must have 1) a gate card stating that he has been okayed in his lessons through the starting gate and 2) x-rays showing that his knees have grown shut. Closed knees are an indication that the animal is physically mature enough to take the strain of racing.

Unless you are phenomenally lucky, the first few races of an untried horse will fall under the unpalatable heading of schooling races. The typical two-year-old is totally bewildered by the people, the noise and the crush of running horses. He could probably use a race or two just to tuck himself up into prime physical condition. Most folks say that a race will strengthen a horse to go half a furlong farther next time out. Some even believe that one race is worth four to six works.

Two-year-old races come packed with frustration for owners and bettors, even though undeniable excitement greets the appearance of two-year-olds flooding the racetracks each autumn. Take heart, the upcoming three-year-old season is the sweetest one of all.

Racing Secretaries make a point of carding plenty of "three-year-olds only" races for the first three quarters of each year. Protected from running against big, bad older horses, the competition can turn up relatively soft. But after this honeymoon, the fields are wide open, which means that horses tend to fall dramatically in class between their three- and four-year-old seasons, when they graduate into competition against the hard-knocking veterans.

Horses will peak physically at seven or eight, but few horses can stay raceworthy that long. The standard cutoff date for a racing career, which only a microscopic proportion of horses ever reach, is about 10 years from year of first start, and it varies from track to track. A horse might live to 30, but 20 is a ripe old age.

On the whole, people seem to be waiting longer before hustling young horses onto the track. Perhaps they feel that not only will these horses be stronger and more coordinated later on, but that a more mature horse will not waste as many races with green antics. Every race takes a toll. Make it count. Cumulative injuries from the wear and tear of racing can keep a wayward student from ever reaching his potential.

HOME CARE

Records

Protect your investment. Running a breeding operation takes organization. If you plan on boarding your breeding stock at one of the larger farms, you can usually rely on them to keep on top of the worming schedule, shot requirements and hoof care for your animal. But even then, you should have some inkling of what is involved so that you can be sure that the farm management is doing things right. A good way to keep all these details straight is to devise individual charts which tell at a glance what has and hasn't been done. (See Appendix.)

Handling

Workers. New horsemen interested in setting up a home-based farm operation would probably do best to concentrate on broodmares and pre-racing stock. These animals have the advantage of needing less sophisticated stable help and it's relatively easy to find people with a background in pleasure horses who can handle the job. Most broodmares are gentle cattle. Babies can be as wild as deer, but they are usually too small to do real damage.

While the reward of a job well done is to have done it yourself, don't try to go it alone with your stable if you have no experience with horses. If you are hesitant or afraid, these animals will be quick to pick up on it. Horses may be less intelligent than pigs, but they are sensitive to the chain of command. One trick of confidence that often works well is to avoid looking directly at a rogue: whenever a horse can discover accommodation in your eyes, he'll know he's got you. If you learn to act impersonal and efficient that horse will generally respond in a businesslike fashion.

Young stock will benefit from being handled—intelligently—by all sorts of people. You'll want to get plenty of stable help, with substitute workers on call. You need people who are relaxed around horses, but willing to work. The combination is elusive. Casual grooms can be as lazy as sin; perfectionists are nervous sorts.

As owner-manager, expect to do plenty of supervising and inspecting because in any horse operation things can spin out of control on eagle's wings. Besides, people always put out more effort when the boss is around, and that goes for veterinarians and farriers, too. Show that you care about your employees as well as the horses and be ready to roll up your sleeves and help. When you pay well, you've got the right to demand good work. No more nagging and scolding. Just warn, dock and fire.

Few commercial farms have time to give the kind of personal care which will make your home operation worthwhile. Once your set-up is kink-free, not only should more of your horses make it to the races, but chances are they may make it several steps higher and last there longer.

Barnwork Checklist for a Winter's Evening

1) Check clipboard for any instructions and sign in.

2) Clean stalls.

3) Put in fresh feed, water and hay.

4) Pony's paddock: rake up old hay, scatter manure, put in fresh water and hay.

5) Bring in horses. Keep stall doors shut—don't trust stall guards to prevent horses from slipping out.

6) Groom each horse.

7) Prepare breakfasts and cover. Be sure there's enough hay brought down for the morning.

8) Sweep barn aisle, tack and feed rooms.

9) Check that all gates and doors are secure, lights turned out.

10) Sign out: time and comments (for example, note which supplies are running low).

Optional

1) School weanlings and yearlings.

2) Odd jobs: move back manure pile; clean water troughs; pick up field stones; scatter manure in fields; clean tubs, buckets and tack; straighten loft, tack and feed rooms.

COORDINATE EXTRA WORK WITH BARN FOREMAN.

The All–Purpose Pony. A good pony puts you on easy street. He can help school, wean and babysit just by being there. But check out his personality before putting him in with expensive stock. Kicking and biting are not his job.

Smaller ponies pose less of a threat and are more quickly accepted by broodmares, who sometimes take them on like foals. The only drawback is that little ponies stand to "founder" on rich pastures. This condition is also known as laminitis and can be brought on by any kind of stress. It easily happens to horses that overindulge, and ponies manage to arrive at the stuffed stage fast. Butterball weight and the strain on their digestive system can start a painful syndrome: hooves grow hot and sore and begin to flatten. Cold water soakings, painkillers and a starvation diet are standard redress.

Forestall foundering by pulling your pony out of springtime pastures. If you have designed an adjoining paddock or enclosed lane next to a pasture, you'll be able to keep the pony healthy year-round while he maintains his over-the-fence friendships.

Layout. Remember that you are raising Thoroughbred horses, not cows. Don't go in for cattle guards, barb wire or all-electric fencing. Spooked horses don't pay much attention to what they are running through unless it is a solid obstacle before their eyes. That's why you must build yourself stout fences with the fence posts placed outside of the rails. Most fences are built the other way around with the post hidden inside the fence. They may look prettier, but rest assured that every lummox will try to push out the rails and bang up his knees on the posts.

White fences are trouble. Advocates say white paint helps horses see fences at night. Big deal. They fade and peel and manage to look shabby no matter how much you invest in time, labor and buckets of paint. With creosote stain, the wood is preserved and any fading is gradual and natural. You'll have kept the sylvan look; no hospital-white legions are marching across your land.

The traditional farm has fields scattered haphazardly around the barn, which means that bringing horses in and out entails walking across driveways and wide open spaces. If you are given the chance to design your own layout on a new farm, keep as much fencing between your horses and the countryside as possible. Enclosed lanes running from the barn to the various fields will help make your life trouble-free.

As mentioned earlier, these lanes will see a lot of pony wear. They're also a great place to store injured horses. Your patients can then enjoy fresh air and fun in the sun without having enough space to run free and reinjure themselves. What's more, paddocks and lanes make perfect temporary quarters for new horses so that your stock can get acquainted before being turned out together. Horses are clannish and territorial. Ostracism might be their least cutting welcome.

Don't forget to be on the lookout for killer trees when plotting the course of your fencing. Horses will nibble and tear off anything within reach to break the monotony of waiting for the next meal. Red maple, yew shrubbery and Kentucky cherry trees all fly the skull and cross bones.

Safety. Safety should be a big preoccupation around a Thoroughbred stable. Let your grooms know that leaving a gate or door unlatched is a sackable act. Young horses excel at getting loose and catching them will be the most frustrating race you'll ever run. Sometimes it can't be helped. Horses will jump over fences and stall doors, even go through them.

You might want to introduce your animals to a taste for carrots because then you'll have something special they will come to you for, should they get loose. Keep the carrots at a minimum or you'll find that some horses will get nippy and nasty whenever you don't give them any. It's like spoiling children with candy.

Horses can lunge, bite and kick. The best cure for anti-social habits is to shout down the offender, although normally your voice should be kept low. Noise will momentarily stun any horse into submission as long as his hearing hasn't been numbed by the groom's country western radio program. Never strike a horse—you won't win in a physical contest.

Dress your animals in leather halters. Be sure to stock extras in all sizes since the beauty and expense of these halters is that they break so easily. Horses can kill themselves in an unbreakable nylon halter if they get it caught on a hoof or metal fixture.

You have got to insist that your help carries a shank when leading the horses in and out, one by one. Horses can easily twist free if grabbed by the halter; having a horse on each hand flushes away what's left of your control. You just never know what a horse can see with his panovision eyes that will start his nostrils quivering.

Whenever a horse does rear back on you, don't pull hard on the lead shank because then he'll have something to brace against. Instead, stand aside and give him a little more line. Watch him topple.

It's not a bad idea to get your horses used to having a chain looped through the halter over the nose. Horses are fairly sensitive to downward pressure behind the ears and a chain nipping the nose bones reinforces your control that much more. A sharp jerk will bring a horse quickly to his senses, so that he doesn't kill himself or you.

Doctoring. Horse accidents will inevitably happen. Have on hand painkilling tablets, sponges, mild soap, peroxide, salves, gauze pads, cotton wrap and bandages, as well as all the injection paraphenalia. If the wound is ugly and you can get a vet right away, it might be better not to mess with it.

Cuts on the lower leg are a special worry. Chances go sky high that they will get infected. Immediate hosing helps clean, anesthesize and bring down the swelling, but you shouldn't rely entirely on home treatment. Call help.

Horses suffering from injuries or illness go down fast. The best indication that something is wrong comes when a horse backs off his feed. This is the time to take out the thermometer, insert it into the rectum and leave it there for three minutes. Normal temperature is around 100°. Always have your thermometer tied to a string with a clothespin attached so that you can clip it to the tail to prevent it from disappearing.

You can bet that disposable syringes, needles and vials of anti-biotics or heavy-duty painkillers will be needed in a panic from time to time. Giving horses intramuscular injections is simple, and you can learn to do it yourself. The middle of the neck is the best spot for an injection. Grab an inch of flesh and stick the needle in first, pull it back 1/8 inch to make sure there's no blood on it signifying that you've hit a vessel, then insert the syringe and push the plunger.

Most older horses don't give a damn about what you're doing, but to be on the safe side, use a "twitch" for difficult cases. This catches the soft flesh of the nose in a leather loop which extends from what looks like an axe handle. When you twist the loop tight, it's either very distracting or quite comforting in an acupressure way.

Hoofwork. If at all possible, give your horses daily grooming sessions. Teaching babies to stand still while tied up takes its toll on halters. Picking up and picking out their feet takes a toll on grooms. A helper to hold up one front leg usually cuts down on the kicking, although you can run into an occasional mean streak which will lash out with all four feet off the ground.

Summon a farrier about every six weeks to trim off the excess hoof growth. If there's any tendency to toe in or out, dig up the best guy around to keep the hooves filed into delicate alignment. Yearlings can sometimes be helped by nailing on shoes in front to counteract nature and help wayward leg bones grow straight.

Setting up Shop. The wish list for a new barn depends on how elaborate your operation will be. Try to find the happy mean between Spendthrift Farm and a rathole.

Consider the basics. Stock plenty of hard rubber buckets as well as feed tubs. Winter freezes water and you'll need something durable that you can toss around to crack out the ice. Mechanized waterers are fretful things and usually don't merit the cost. As for the fields, troughs need constant cleaning and refilling, underground plumbing is expensive. The best solution is to loop your fences over year-round streams and let nature do the watering.

Along with putting in a supply of nuts and bolts hardware, remember to buy plenty of two-ended snaps or their handy counterparts which are designed to defy freezing up. You'll eventually need to hook together everything in sight.

Any farmboy knows the tools of the trade. Pitchforks, shovels and a couple of wheelbarrows. Suit yourself about buying tractors and a complete range of farming equipment. It's not entirely necessary because custom farmers can easily be found to do the heavy work. Seems like more fun to put your time and big money into horses.

Lofts are lofts. But make sure there's an easy way to load up the hay and straw. If the barn doors are built high enough, a truck can drive right in.

Tin-lined feed bins help keep out water and rodents. In warm weather, you always have to be on the lookout for moisture-caused mold. Mice, rats and woods creatures love a barn year-round, but a troop of vigilante cats will make them head home. Bait sends them heavenbound. The only thing you'll want to get into your feed is a feed scoop, preferably indestructible.

Whatever else you do, your horses will be eternally grateful to you for the latest state-of-the-art fly control for summer sanity. Sprays, repellents, pellets, cattle tags, wasps, electrocuters. Whatever works is worth using. If you have an airy barn, shutting the horses up nice and cool during the day will give them some peace as long as the manure pile is kept down and the doorway leading to it closed.

Fill your tackroom with grooming supplies, medical whatnot and a twitch for good behavior. Your tack needs will be easy: leather halters in all sizes. Lead shanks and lunge lines. If you're into breaking yearlings or know a teacher who makes house calls, you might find room for a racing bridle with rubberized reins and a light exercise saddle.

Your stalls should be spacious but closed with full-length or yoke grids to inhibit jumpers. You may want to get some outside advice on what kind of stall surface drains best in your area. The fun finally begins when you're ready to rig up stall guards and any number of personalized touches just like the fancier shedrows. But don't forget to treat yourself first to a leak-proof pair of all-weather boots.

Winterizing. Anywhere south of Alaska, you'll rarely need to blanket your stock overnight if straw bedding is laid down nice and thick. Horses that go outside every day, freeze or rain, will grow their own overcoats anyway. Long manes look fine if kept combed, and are useful for warmth in the winter as well as for keeping away summertime flies.

Shagginess prepares a broodmare well for shipping mid-winter to the large breeding farms which leave horses outside around the clock with only a run-in shed as shelter against the elements. This system is basically a labor-saving device, but some horsemen will swear that it actually keeps horses healthier since it is more in line with their natural environment. To be honest, the practice of bringing horses in part-time is not entirely based on humane concerns either. Horses benefit from handling, schooling and getting used to the general stable environment. A field-raised horse can go berserk when he is confined for the first time to a shedrow stall.

Showing. Because racehorse owners are such a competitive lot, it won't be long before you'll want to branch out into show competition. An outfit with a hand in breeding is always tempted to steal some laurels in the stock classes at summer horse shows. Be realistic. It's hard work to organize, school and groom your entrants to perfection, and you'll often be pitted against the top professionals in the showhorse field. Shows are big business for these horsemen. They are counting on blue ribbons to sell their horses and enhance their reputations.

©DAILY RACING FORM

Plan ahead. Complete all the paperwork. Get your horses used to wearing a show bridle early so they won't chomp on it inelegantly. Practice their walking, trotting, backing up and positioning. Bathe, pull manes and shave whiskers, ears and fetlocks days beforehand. Everything has to be braided on showday to look nice, but some people make these last minute touches easier with the common, though not quite legal, practice of tranquilizing their horses lightly before the excitement begins. They should save some of the stuff for themselves.

Showing racing stock subjects it to undue risk. Be sure to protect legs when shipping by using boots or bandages. Hire plenty of good help and arrange for a top handler to present your horses. Take only the tallest animals—you're wasting your time with a compact model, regardless of looks. If you can find a midget handler, your horses will loom like giants. That's a tip from auction block tactics.

Be sure to arrive in plenty of time since show schedules are nebulous and underfilled classes can move things up by hours. Watch the earlier classes to get a line on where the highest ground and the most advantageous position can be found. The best handlers will stand on their heads to coax their charges into an alert and graceful stance before the judge's eye. If you're taking a stab at showing your own animals, dress to the teeth and wear a hat. Hats and fistfuls of grass are stock items for entertaining horses.

Upperville. The great-granddaddy of all shows is the Upperville Colt and Horse Show near Middleburg, Virginia. The gracious setting of ancient trees and rickety fences belies the ruthless competition. It is old-world and charmingly disorganized, with spectators drifting among the entrants. The judges are a well-kept secret: everyone manages to assume a hushed judgmental air.

Human activity begets politics. So does equine. But shows like Upperville are getting less partial as a few deserving newcomers have burrowed their way into the clubby atmosphere of the high hat circuit.

Diet

Feed. A quick cure for neurotic behavior is an intelligent and well-balanced diet. Horsemen like to brag a lot and for some reason feeding a high protein commercial mix to farm animals is a point of pride. But chances are that it'll drive the horses wild. The extremely high phosphorous content in most grain proteins can tie up calcium, a mineral essential not only for good bone but for a well-balanced nervous system. Because any excess phosphorous can only be expelled from the body in combination with calcium, if you overfeed protein you'll artificially bring about a calcium deficiency. Balance is the key: rich meals can spawn a host of developmental problems.

Weanlings may legitimately need to gobble up protein, but they seem to be an exception. When horses in other categories show an increased need for protein, nutritionists are finding out that they may simply need more food overall. The proportion of protein in these bigger meals would have to be upped only slightly. For example, in the last three months of pregnancy when the fetus is gaining two-thirds of its birth size, a mare's need for protein will increase by around 15% while her total energy intake requirements will go up by a comparable 12%.

New horsemen always want to hammer down from the very start exactly how much to feed their farm stock. It doesn't work that way. You'll find that scientific studies (read them all!) lead back to the basic tenet, it depends on the horse. Growing animals, broodmares and working stock will naturally need more than the holiday crowd, which should be kept from packing on weight. Horse metabolism is individual. Some run around a lot, others run to fat.

Start out feeding several quart scoops each morning and a few more at night, along with plenty of hay, which can be a good source of calcium as well as protein. Watch closely. Do the horses clean up? Do they ignore the hay and grass? How do they look? Tailor feed rations accordingly. It's an ongoing process and will change with the seasons and with growing spurts.

Supplements. Vitamin and mineral supplements are miracle workers. Some can make horses digest everything so efficiently that they gain weight while eating less, grow excellent hooves and metamorphose from Mr. Hyde into Dr. Jekyll.

Feed salesmen may gripe that feeding supplements is counter-productive as well as expensive. The trouble with that argument is that the man-made supplements already mixed into the commercial feeds can be clumsily formulated. Because nature has a finer hand for balancing nutrients, any seafood meal supplement low in iodine may be what's needed to bridge the nutrition gap.

Good supplements become crucial when you run into a horse that's bent on self-destructing before he reaches the races. These animals usually come with some kind of unconscionable handling in their pasts. For instance, horses who have been weaned with another baby in the same stall can become violently insecure whenever they're left alone. Horses who have never been away from a herd before often behave likewise.

Most nut cases respond nicely when you feed them calcium and magnesium over and above what come naturally in grass and hay. These minerals must work in partnership: calcium soothes the nerve endings while magnesium facilitates muscle contractions and motor control, and seems to prevent any excess calcium from being laid down in tissue. Calcium and magnesium powder, dolomite or bone meal can be ordered through any health food store and mixed into grain with a touch of molasses or oil for recalcitrant eaters. Experiment with a different recipe on grumpy friends or insomniac lovers. The results are evident as soon as the food starts to digest, and unlike chemical sedatives, there are no known side effects.

What helps on the farm is not always what you want for the track. Horses frequently have to get a little wound up to race, snorting fire and billowing smoke. It's probably best to let the trainer feed a product he's used and believes in. If the horses look pestiferous and are doing worse, change trainers as well as supplements.

Incidentally, you'll know when your horses aren't getting enough salt because they'll probably start chewing the wood off all the stalls and fences. You can usually cure this habit by keeping a mineral brick in each feed tub and salt blocks for licking in the fields. It's equally true that gnawing could just be a sign of boredom.

Hay. Hay can be harvested from legume, grass and cereal plants. As for quality, alfalfa is king. Nice and leafy, it has an emerald color and sweet smell. Red clover hay is also a hit and has a slight sedative and laxative effect in the richness of its flowers. A timothy/clover mix does the job, while orchard grass is only of interest to starvelings or gluttons. Forget the rest.

Be careful of second-cutting alfalfa. That's a rich crop with fewer weeds and more leaves. Vets will advise you to mix it with less tasty hay. It's something like feeding your horses too much chocolate. To circumvent the digestion problem, opt for first-cutting alfalfa which is high in protein, but stemmier so that horses won't wolf it down.

The season's first hay crop usually comes in mid-June. If you're like everyone else, last year's stock will have run low and you'll rush out to buy the decent new stuff. But remember that most barn lofts heat up fast in summer, and hay will store that heat. What's worse, alfalfa can mildew easily during warm, muggy weather. Try to buy only your immediate needs until the end of the summer when you can stock up for the year at a fair enough price.

Alfalfa hay in particular must be cured for a few weeks before using it. This process is more graphically called allowing the hay to "sweat" or dry out completely. Only if the hay has been harvested under the optimum weather conditions of sunshine and low humidity can you safely bypass the curing process. If you're in a hurry to use an uncured bale, split one open and let the leaves dry out for 24 hours.

Hay can be sold by the bale or by the ton. The rule of thumb is 40 bales to the ton, and the price drops with the bigger orders. Trackmen end up paying a premium for everything, especially hay, since shedrow storage space is always minimal.

Grass. Fresh spring grass is life-sustaining. Horses say there's nothing better, although owners of performance animals hedge their bets by continuing to feed grain and hay.

Agricultural consultants abound to tell you how to turn trash into blue grass and red clover. Stay away from fescue grass. It stands accused of causing broodmares to abort, because it seems to be susceptible to a harmful fungus as well as being low in selenium. Clover is thought to offset fescue toxicity.

Maintaining pastures is an ongoing cycle and needs regular testing, fertilizing, weeding and seeding. When results become self-defeating and the field chokes on its own prosperity, you might want to run in some cattle to clean it up.

Vet Work

Worming. The most important on-going health consideration is the control of internal parasites. Worming is normally done on a flexible two-month basis, although some ideas are in the offing about devising new worming schedules which would concentrate on spring and tackle the growing resistance of parasites to wormers. Farms always worm new horses upon arrival as a precaution against importing undesirables. Uncontrolled worms are horribly debilitating and some can be the basis for a deadly colic. Colic of any sort is the greatest killer of mature horses.

One theory of worming is to disrupt the life cycle of parasites which live part-time in the host animal. Worming pastes marketed under various brand names can be handily squeezed into the throat of a horse so that he has no choice but to gulp 'em down. These pastes should be alternated with the old-fashioned method of tube worming. This calls for stuffing a rubber hose down a horse's gullet to his stomach to ensure a direct hit and pouring in a particularly effective worming compound.

The new kid on the block is ivermectin, and horsemen are standing by to see just how tough it really is. The injection has sort of a fungus base which paralyzes the enemy and gives effective protection for a good ten weeks against the parasites in every stage of maturity throughout the host. It should probably be rotated with other paste or tube drenching preparations.

Colic. Bloodworm larvae can bring on a raging colic if they are allowed to migrate into the blood vessels of the intestinal tract. They will damage the arteries and obstruct the blood supply so that bowel movement slows to a crawl. When a horse's digestive system shuts down, the hay and grain in the pipeline start to ferment. Horses are not designed to burp or vomit, and the pressure can build to an excruciating rupture point.

The first priority is to relieve the pain, then to get things moving along. Painkillers and muscle relaxants help cut down on the stress, but the time-honored trick is to lower a rubber tube into the stomach to relieve gas build-up. Mineral oil can now be pumped in and the horse's belly monitored for the hoped-for signs of intestinal rumbling and imminent defecation.

The stricken animal should be walked until these remedies start taking effect to keep him from rolling and thrashing around, and possibly ending up with a fatally twisted gut. To speed things along, the doctor might even want to reach far in through the rectum to feel for any obstructions, but only a bionic vet can be expected to tunnel along a hundred feet of intestine. As a final touch, the vet will probably give his patient multiple doses of wormer to flush out offending parasites if he suspects that they caused the problem in the first place.

Colic can be brought on by so many things in addition to worms—moldy hay, a change in weather, sandy stream water—that most of the time you go ahead and treat the symptoms without ever really knowing what caused it. Some equine insurance companies take colic seriously enough to consider its appearance in a medical history as a sign of inherent weakness and good reason to rule a horse off their insurable list.

Foal Follies. Each foal should start his shot and worming schedule when two months old. Tetanus shots and boosters are usually the first to be given and are repeated yearly throughout the horse's life. After six months of age, these animals can be given basically the same immunization program as an adult horse. This would cover vaccinations against several cold-like infections as well as more exotic ones against rabies and sleeping sickness, if these diseases are locally prevalent. (See Appendix.)

The huge breeding farms routinely throw more medication at their horses more often because any contagious outbreak could spell disaster. This elephant gun approach brings with it the danger of toxins building up, particularly from overzealous worming, so be sure to pin your vet down on exactly what's called for in your particular area, and no more.

Vets will tell you not to worry about sniffles in young horses as long as they don't cough. It seems that every horse that goes through an auction comes down with a cold as a result of the stress. It spreads at a gallop. An old-time remedy is cod liver oil which is high in vitamin A. This promotes the impermeability of the mucous membrane against invading germs. Lace it liberally with molasses and they'll lick their troughs clean.

Coggins Test. Every horse that expects to come in contact with other horses in racing, showing or travelling is required to have a certificate which verifies that he has been tested and found negative for equine infectious anemia. This certificate is known as a "negative coggins." How recently this test needs to have been made—within six months or within one year—is a varying requirement which does its share to sow gray hair on a horseman's pelt. The results of the blood test can sometimes take a good two weeks to be received and typically arrive long after the big event they were needed for. Aside from the inconvenience, there are scattered protests about how really necessary the whole process is. The angriest detractors are those who've had to put down a nice animal that tested positive, but was obviously not suffering from the disease nor appeared to be particularly contagious.

REGISTRATION

The Jockey Club

As the ruling body for Thoroughbred racing, membership in the Jockey Club reflects racing's heritage of wealthy and venerable patrons. It does not include jockeys.

The New York Jockey Club and its branch in Kentucky divide their functions in mysterious ways. It seems that New York primarily handles new registrations and name claims, while the Kentucky office mans the giant computers which churn out statistics on race and produce records. Both sections are unfailingly helpful, if periodically overworked. What's more, New York's News Service Bureau can be counted on as a fountainhead of racing lore.

There are a few forms to fill out and procedures to follow to make your horse eligible for the track or breeding shed. Never too many, since the Jockey Club must have realized that literacy is not a strong point among horsemen.

On Sight. The Jockey Club is basically more interested in bloodlines than in markings when qualifying horses for registration. In contrast, Quarter Horse registration rules can ban markings they consider ugly such as a bald face with the white extending farther than the corner of the upper lip. The Jockey Club's true concern with appearance is how it relates to the correct identification of every Thoroughbred.

Most racehorses are bays. In the summer they become bright coppery brown with black points, meaning the mane, tail and lower legs. For confusion's sake, these coats turn dark brown in the winter. There are also year-round brown horses and chestnut horses ranging in hue from golden to liver. Greys generally start out darker at birth and end up snow-white with sexy kohl-like markings around their eyes. Roans throw some red hairs in with the white over much of their bodies, though it may take a microscope to find them.

Standing all alone is the black, sleek and mean, defining the breed. To be on the safe side, he may be officially dubbed dark-brown. No matter how you call it, he's still the one who inspires the storytellers.

Heads come with stars, stripes, nose snips and bald-faces. Powder noses are mainly seasonal. Legs may be marked with white coronets, pasterns, ankles and stockings. Sometimes a dark spot will show up here or there on a white coronet.

Moroccan legend has it that a white spot on the off (right) hind leg is the sure sign of swiftness. Despite this, markings seem to have minimal effect on racing performance. You can safely ignore the chant, "four white feet and a blaze on the nose, hit 'em with a shovel and feed 'em to the crows." These markings may have been quintessentially unlucky for some, but Northern Dancer's great son, The Minstrel, seems to have overcome them in style. He was Europe's Horse of the Year at three after he won the Epsom Derby, the Irish Sweeps Derby and the King George VI and Queen Elizabeth Diamond Stakes.

Because Thoroughbreds come in so few basic colors and such a limited range of markings, the Jockey Club experiments now and then with photographing night-eyes for better identification. Also known as "chestnuts," these wart-like growths on the inside of a horse's leg are as individual as fingerprints. Their beauty is that they don't lose their size or shape over the lifetime of a mature horse.

The Ropes. Application forms for registering a foal are simple but must be accompanied by the stallion certificate, pictures, a description of markings and hair whorls and, of course, a check. The fee grows progressively higher for registering Thoroughbreds at later stages which is an incentive for the breeder to get his act together on time.

You should automatically receive the stallion cover certificate for your new foal provided you've remembered to pay the stud fee. This ought to be negotiated into falling due when a foal stands and nurses. The "live foal" condition used to be universal until some stallion owners got a little greedy and began asking for an advance stud fee payment in September, months before the foaling date in spring. With mares now in clamorous demand to fill the books of all but the most prestigious stallions, there is plenty of room for wheeling and dealing. Few horsemen pay the asked-for price and still fewer pay on time.

The Jockey Club, through its National Horse Identification Program, has trained a cadre of professional horse identifiers that charges a nominal fee to take the required pictures, describe the markings and fill in the rest of the forms for you. The markings submitted for the registration certificate must fit the horse to a "T," otherwise track officials will refuse to tattoo the registration number under a horse's front lip when he comes of racing age. These numbers are meticulously checked by a horse identifier before each race.

Not only has the Jockey Club worked hard to find the most foolproof guidelines for visually identifying racehorses, it has also turned its hand to inaugurating blood tests for ascertaining lines of breeding. All Thoroughbred sires and mares newly bought or brought to stud are now required to get on the blood-type record. Eventually every foal will be routinely blood-typed.

State-bred Programs

While you're getting your foal papers in order, be sure to find out if you're eligible to apply for registration in a state breeding incentive program. Most of these bonus programs are funded from the parimutuel take, but that's where the uniformity ends. States have individualistic twists to the definition of what constitutes a state-bred foal: parentage, ownership or place of birth. Sign up wherever your stock qualifies—these programs mean money.

In some states, healthy sums are paid out to the owner, breeder and stallion owner every time a registered state-bred does well in a race run at any track in that state. These set percentages of the purses are added on top of regular purse winnings to encourage horsemen not only to breed to in-state stallions, but to race in that state as well.

Special races restricted to state-breds can also be a big come-on for the local breeding industry. The pots are sweet and the competition relatively weak.

Incentive programs are taken seriously. When you stand to make royalties of something like 40% of the purses won by your homebreds, it's going to make you shop and compare before signing a stallion contract or setting up store. The competition among states to seduce breeding interests is paying off all around. Horsemen are humming and state economies are getting a boost; it's a boom time for foals.

Breeders' Cup Series. The most flamboyant national and international scheme of incentive awards comes wrapped in the Breeders' Cup Series. Stallions must pay stiff fees to get on the eligible list, while their offspring are also nicked for cold, hard cash—U.S. funds only. In one orgiastic day described as the World Series of racing, half this loot will be flung out in millions of dollars worth of race purses. The other half will be used to gild the purses of long-established stakes races whenever a lucky nominee comes in first, second or third. Both nominators and owners stand to get wildcat rich off just one nice animal.

Silks

Many state racing commissions automatically register your colors when you apply for an owner's license, so that you will probably already have your silks lined up by the time your first homebred makes it to the track. The uniquely convoluted process of getting silks okayed by the Jockey Club for racing in the Big Apple also ought to be looked into early in the game just in case you're growing yourself a prodigy. Shoot for the stars.

The Jockey Club does what it can to help horsemen register silks quickly when they intend to ship in a big horse right away. *If* the colors meet the official criteria and *if* they have not already been reserved. When problems arise, you can use the house colors—dismal grey or wretched blue—as a one-time thing as long as you register at the time of the NYRA race.

Silks are your signature. In registering new silks, the Jockey Club is a rigorous arbiter of taste. It knows a thing or two about style. No more than four colors are allowed, two on the bodice and two on the sleeves. Knick-knacks and doodads are held within limits. Keep it simple, keep it striking.

The stumbling block is there are just "x" number of simple combinations around and thousands of owners. Consequently, your design submissions can be rejected time after time until you get lucky and get it right.

Names

Foal registration forms are sent out around July of each year, but you may want to request reservation of a foal's name long before then. The Jockey Club publishes a book of names currently in use and has a die-hard set of criteria on what is acceptable. With some 45,000 foals being dropped in spring, you'll have to look pretty far afield for originality. (See Appendix.)

The fillip in breeding or buying young stock is that you can name it yourself. Think big: imagine the name headlining the *RACING FORM*. Single-word names have the most panache. Cute derivatives of the horse parents' names are sometimes nauseating and rarely more appealing than the idea of Jr. tacked onto a man's name. Foreign words are a great source of the exotic and new, but will make you few friends among track announcers.

Honor the dignity of a racehorse with a worthy name. Make it heroic or make it catchy, but don't make it dumb or insulting. "Mighty Slow" could be a self-fulfilling prophecy. The Arabs know that in naming a horse you give it a soul.

GELDING THE LILY

The colt by Fast Hilarious was bred okay, but strangely put together and kind of a runt. Trusting beginners' luck, we saw in him the prodigy who would carry our silks Derby-bound in triumph. Enthusiasm ignited our minds and we named the horse Fast Harro in honor of father Harro, a swashbuckling cavalry officer in all his baronial splendor.

It is hard enough to chart a decent course with your own ego entwined in a horse's destiny. It is murderous to compound this folly by adding on a giant one.

Fortunately the cold, deep Atlantic was between us when we told the old man that Fast Harro's sex life had been cut short and ceremoniously flung onto the shedrow roof. From then on it was world-weary sighs as the inevitable revelations of Fast Harro's negligible talent came to pass, and all the initial thrill ebbed out to sea.

○ Chapter Four ○

TRAITS

SWAN SONG

Singing Susan. Once there was a little filly for sale who had calves' knees. Nobody would touch her except some nut who had $29,000 in his back pocket. She grew out of it a bit, went on to win stakes with awesome ease. The *FORM* said she'd been resold for 900 grand when her foreleg shattered.

Achilles' knees. They're like time bombs.

Sharjah. In another land there was a pony, er, racehorse, who looked pretty bad. He was squatty and heavily boned. The pasterns in back were near parallel to the ground.

"It's just the fur and the fat. He'll grow soon, you'll see."

He grew up to be dumpy and slow. True to form. This one is closer to home.

THE MEAT OF THE MATTER

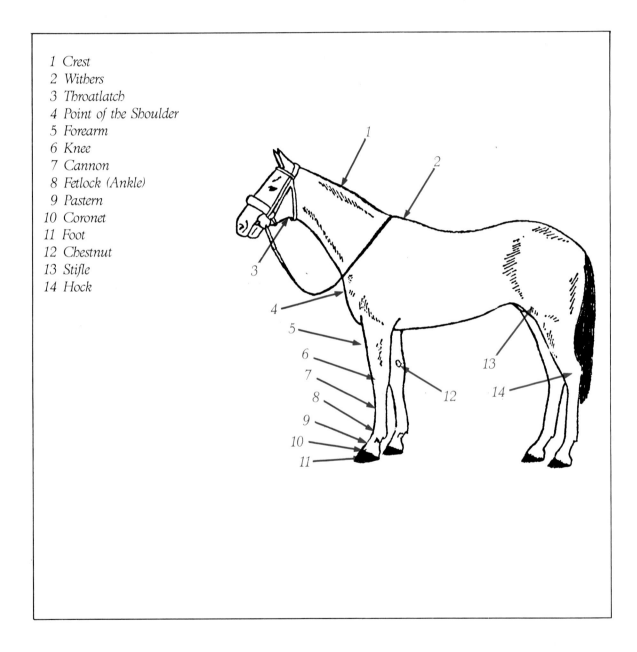

1 Crest
2 Withers
3 Throatlatch
4 Point of the Shoulder
5 Forearm
6 Knee
7 Cannon
8 Fetlock (Ankle)
9 Pastern
10 Coronet
11 Foot
12 Chestnut
13 Stifle
14 Hock

CONFORMATION

There's no getting around a discussion of conformation, but it will be painless. Since there are few perfect racehorses, the trick is to recognize which faults you can live with and which might preclude a long and useful racing career.

Bear in mind that sometimes it's the conformation aberration which makes the champion racehorse. Take the compactness of Northern Dancer. This was once considered a fault. Since being pressed into stud, he has advanced the evolution of the Thoroughbred on a worldwide basis as a tribute to his ability to uncoil as fast as a tightly wound spring. That's why you should weigh the dos and don'ts of conformation less in terms of aesthetics and more on how they jibe with the mechanics of running.

After you've seen a few hundred racehorses, conformation quirks will automatically jump out at you. The ground rules of racing conformation are that the front legs make or break a racehorse. They catch hell from bearing over two-thirds of the body's weight.

Looking at a horse head-on, a plumb line should be able to bisect each leg perfectly with no toeing in or out. Toeing out begets a wasted motion known as "winging" and carries with it the probability that the front legs will lash each other in flight. Those who toe in, as well as floppy-eared horses, are supposed to make good jumpers, but that doesn't help much on the racetrack. Toeing in makes a horse land on the outside rim of his foot, precipitating an awkward paddling motion.

In the best of all worlds, you should be able to put a prospective purchase through his paces. A horse's motion or way of going is as revealing as his standing-still conformation. Leg action in all the gaits points up not only conformation faults and injuries, but, occasionally, a bright spot of talent. The ideal horse hydroplanes along with precious little kneefold or effort, resulting in the greatest conservation of energy.

At a walk, a horse that's a little sore will be slightly "off" and move his weight unevenly. When a horse bobs his head and neck with every stride ("Good morning, good morning!"), you know he's got problems. During a canter or gallop, you'd have to look pretty closely to tell if a horse isn't striding out or is coming down hard, but trotting or jogging a sore horse is a dead giveaway. At this pace, a horse will definitely favor his hurt limb. That's why jockeys will always please their trainers by trotting as little as possible before pulling up to dismount, just in case the track vet or potential claiming interests are looking on. You can bet that anyone active in the claiming game makes a point of scanning each interesting racehorse to see how he comes out of a race.

Back at a standstill, you'll want to scrutinize the front legs in profile. Horsemen learn in elementary school to look for a 45° slope to the front pasterns, the bones between the ankle and hoof. (This slope should be repeated in the angle of the hooves and the shoulder.) Pasterns are shock absorbers. With pasterns that are

'HE WAS BRED BY YOUR FATHER?'

short and upright, there's not enough protective springiness, although these horses tend to be speedy. At the other extreme, very long and sloping pasterns indicate that a horse will have a slower and weaker push-off action.

You should look for a short cannon bone specifically in the front legs. Interestingly enough, horse legs have almost no muscle below the knee so you won't want to have too much lower leg for the upper arm to haul around. The sheath of tendons enveloping the lower leg should be visibly defined and well-attached, not "tied-in," that is, radically indented just under the back of the knee.

The next lesson in a horseman's primer is that a horse should be neither "buck-kneed" (knees slightly bent) nor "calf-kneed" (knees set back). Buck knees are also known as "bench knees" or being "over-in-the-knees." While not desirable, they are endurable. Calf-knees are always bad; they are prime candidates for snapping. The landing stress put on an over-extended knee joint would bend it backward with the pressure of a catapult. Makes them fast, but frightening.

Any good handbook or horseman can clue you in on an endless amount of exotica about equine forelegs. If these forelegs pass all your tests, move on to the shoulder which should slope in a long diagonal from the beginning of a horse's back (the "withers") to the lower breast. A horse's reach when his front leg is extended will be parallel to that line. A good reach with a short back and lengthy undercarriage indicates a nice long stride. A sharp, near vertical shoulder angle would effectively limit this stride. Man O'War was perfect at 24 feet; ultranew Sports-medicine training methods promise a 27-foot stretch.

Much tripe has been written about the characteristics sought in a horse's neck and head. Horses with scrawny necks and ratty heads do just fine on the track, but it's true that the more attractive features seem the best designed for conveying plenty of air to the lungs. Look for a large nostril and a throatlatch big enough to let you place at least four fingers under the head between the jaw bones. A nicely sculptured neck and head will also provide a working counter-balance for the motion of the body.

Nobody should laugh at swaybacks because some of them can run. But these animals seem to enjoy rolling on their backs more than most, which shows there must be discomfort and weakness going along with the loose linkage. Incidentally, any horse who rolls in a stall runs the risk of getting "cast" or wedged up against the side of the stall. A horse will fight desperately to get free and the struggle could leave him with a fatally twisted gut.

The height of a horse is really not a problem as long as a horse is well-balanced. The rule of thumb for years was to pick the taller horse over the short, but any race handicapper would lose his shirt on these grounds. The fact is that largeness tends to emphasize faults—there's more weight hitting on a weak point.

Robust little Northern Dancer is the best argument that winners come in all sizes. Horses are measured in "hands" of four inches each to the withers. A good-sized horse comes in at 16 hands. Northern Dancer looks at least a hand smaller, but happens to be perfectly slapped together. Short-coupled horses can sometimes make up in quick accelerating ability what they might lack in a long stride.

It is important that a horse's backlegs be well under him. Site an imaginery plumb line running from the back of the rump, through the hock and cannon bone to the ground. Horses are actually four-wheel drive, but since the hind quarters push the horse out of the starting gate, they help generate early speed. If the legs are set so far back that they look like the stretch position of a Tennessee Walker, an animal obviously can't get the same lift-off. Some horsemen love a sickle-hocked sprinter whose back legs slant under his body at a stand. They reason that these legs will hit the ground in an especially wide arc, transmitting speed from a big push-off. There's universal doubt, though, that sickle-hocks would have strength when called on to provide most of the on-going propulsion.

Hooves should be in an attractive proportion to the rest of the horse. Most horsemen go in for a nice, big foot as a way of covering ground faster and more efficiently, provided it's not out-sized and clumsy. Large hooves are supposed to be a sure-fire sign of a good turfer.

Small, misshapen feet should make you wary. They signal that a lot of corrective trimming and shoeing could have been done to make a horse's legs appear straight. Corrective hoof work is okay on young animals when a little more taken off this side or that can help leg bones grow straight. But once a horse is in training, it's crazy to fool around with his hooves just to make him stand pretty. By this time, the horse's legs have become accustomed to their own natural alignment. Tinkering will cause pain.

The rest of the insights into the ideal horse you've probably already absorbed from watching Trigger on TV. Racehorses come in all sizes and shapes, and are often not so very different from other breeds despite what the Thoroughbred chauvinists say. Good sprinters may look suspiciously like Quarter Horses—muscle-bound with huge hind ends, thick chests and short legs. Distance horses run more to form. They are usually rangier and elegant, with a classically English line.

For several decades in this century, England's racetracks would not allow mongrelized American Thoroughbreds to race in that country. This got its start after most American tracks everywhere but Kentucky and Maryland were shut down in a muckraking fervor during the early 1900s. The onslaught of U.S. horses shipped off to England precipitated a xenophobic reaction known as the Jersey Act, which ended up barring from racing any Thoroughbred who could not trace his ancestry to Weatherby's Stud Book. The vagaries of life in the Colonies and the dislocations of the Civil War made pedigree anyone's guess.

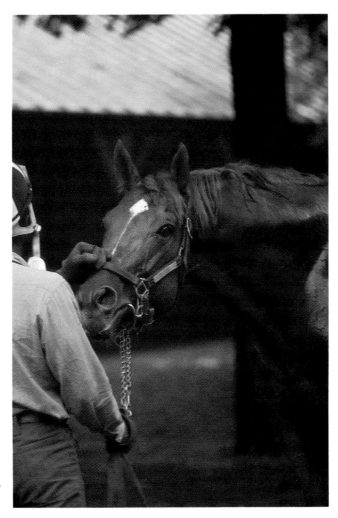

"Sexy"

Although racing was gradually resumed in many states, it was not until 1949 that Britain's restrictive statutes were taken off the books. Ironically, the best and most prized racehorses in the world today have evolved from our democratic melting pot. Horsemen on both sides of the Atlantic now realize that there are no ugly or ill-bred horses in the winner's circle.

Once you've learned conformation, the terms and, in time, the refinements, you can file it away in the back of your mind. You'll need it mainly to cultivate a sense of savoir faire and to make unhurried examinations of auction stock and private buys. On those occasions, a horseman can reinforce his trained eye by putting to use his callous paws to seek heat and flex joints. Applying even pressure, he should work his hands all the way down each suspect leg looking for tenderness and filling. A sound horse won't particularly mind—the last would-be buyer felt the same.

When you're about to claim a horse, though, conformation faults come in a poor third behind past performances and racing injuries. All you'll ever have time for is to let your eyes rove across the horse in a girl-watcher's once-over. Your instincts must carry the day.

PERSONALITY

Although any hardbitten horseman would shrink from the amateurism of attributing human personalities to horses, these animals still manage to come through with a puzzling range of quirks which can ultimately interfere with racing performance. Some ingrained bad habits you just have to work around; others can be drawn off by doing everything possible to give the horse confidence. A happy horse can be counted on to run at least a class better than his cranky stablemate.

The trainer has a few cards to play. He can experiment with feed and supplements to calm a nervous horse or turn a brooder into the cock of the walk. Arrange for a nose-to-tail going over by the vet. Design a sensitive and specific training regime. Hire good help. But more than anything else, he can choose the right race. It works wonders on horse morale.

Owners must realize that there's nothing humiliating about running a horse in a cheap claiming race. If that horse has been running in the gutter, chances are nobody will want to claim him from you at any price. Giving him an easy win could actually be the turning point of his humdrum career. Once a racehorse learns that winning is fun and that the glow of success draws awe and attention, he might just get out of his wheelchair and start running. Then the shedrow will resound with the victorious clinking of Michelobs.

Horses are not the smartest animals, but they can compensate by being exceptionally valiant. Some of the other characteristics you might find appealing in friends and household pets are not always what you are looking for in a racehorse. The best racehorses seem to be single-minded sorts who are not particularly interested in human love and affection. They live to eat and run.

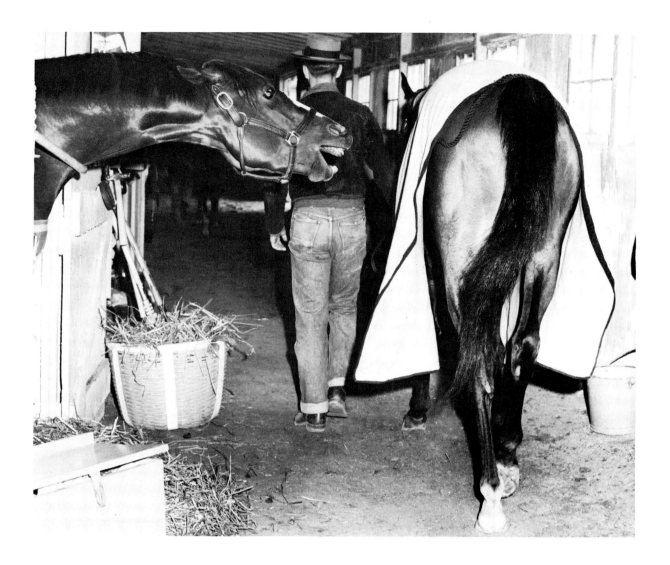

Aggression can be as desirable as talent. It often takes exceptional grittiness to be successful on the track. Bear this in mind with pin-eared and pushy types on the farm. As long as nobody teases them into becoming killers, chances are excellent that they'll grow into tough and useful racehorses.

Every racehorse operates under a time fuse. Not only is per diem expensive and patience short with a difficult student, but every race adds to the aches and pains endured by all professional athletes. A down-right stupid horse (some pedigrees are as notorious for this shortcoming as others are for soft bone) will probably need an unusually long and depressing series of schooling races until he sees the light. It is the same with horses who are not particularly competitive. The whole point of being first escapes them. As a last resort, you might need to hire Dr. Doolittle to whinney a few words in the inveterate maiden's* ear so that he will learn where the finish line is, both on the track and in his life.

Racing is a bottom-line business where it pays to be realistic if you love the sport and want to stay alive. In the infinite variety of horse personalities, either inherited or shaped by the mare's mothering and the general environment, a rotten attitude vis-à-vis racing can be as detrimental as no talent at all. Remember this whenever you are evaluating a horse's worth.

*A maiden is a horse of any age or sex who has never won a race.

PUTTING OUT

King of the Cuff had it all. Good breeding, good looks and a dollop of talent. But he was grumpy, and because of his cross and sulking attitude he was among the cheapest of the cheap claimers.

The Dee-Kay Corral Stable took a shot, claimed him, and dropped him into the hands of a sweet-faced boy with curly, shoulder-length hair. Cuff fell in love. It turned springtime in his heart, his feet grew wings. Instead of clumping out of the starting gate muttering into the flying dirt, this horse was ready to run. Cuff knew his groom was looking on, so he'd catapult to the front leading by lengths and winning once, twice, three times or more.

But love affairs have a way of ending sadly and soon. The groom, unaware of it all, left to sign on with an outfit stabled closer to home.

Sour—that's the only way to describe it. Listless, worldweary and bored. Cuff slid effortlessly down the claiming ladder. Looked like ignominy might be his only claim to lasting fame.

©DAILY RACING FORM

93

○ Chapter Five ○

BUYER BEWARE

96

BUYER
BEWARE

Racing is not a solitary sport. There is plenty of horseplay between owners, trainers, track officials and betting fans, like it or not. The silver lining to all this togetherness is that racing lends itself so easily to entertaining even the most boring friends and clients. It is an unsurpassed memory-maker and a walking, talking conversation piece. An autographed picture of your guest in the winner's circle ranks higher than a Neiman-Marcus Christmas present.

Buying a horse, on the other hand, should be an essentially private affair. You need to be keyed into your own studied preferences and intuitive reactions. Unforgivably bad buys can be made in the hilarity of the moment when you feel spurred on to entertain your audience with a grandstand play.

Splash some cold water on your ego with the thought that all livestock purchases will be a telling reflection of your own good sense and taste. Tune out scuttlebutt. Consider the source: bettors, like bartenders, are notorious know-it-alls who deal advice and lose money with undiluted earnestness.

Another word of caution before buying breeding or racing stock. Most of us are so much in awe of greatness that we will rush to take on over-the-hill stock, hoping to restore it to the grandeur that was Rome. These horses will always be stars, but you'll probably end up with the equine equivalent of a present-day Elizabeth Taylor or Zsa Zsa Gabor.

Whenever you make a bad buy, as will inevitably happen since horses are always a gamble, remember that you do not have to bear the cross of your mistake forever. Unlike relatives and business partners, bad stock can and should be ditched. If you can't absorb this kind of loss either financially or egotistically, you shouldn't be in racing. Your entire write-off will be so much smaller if you can be quick to stop throwing good money after bad. Unproductive stock is not fun and never profitable.

'HAVE YOU EVER SEEN SUCH PERFECT LEGS ?'

PRIVATE DEALS

Try to steer clear of private deals. Usually overpriced, they can come fraught with recriminations. Lacking the relatively impersonal clarity of an auction buy or racetrack claim, the buyer and seller often feel bound together forever in mutual defensiveness over a horse's progress. This is even worse with friends. If the horse succeeds, they'll be annoyed about selling him too cheap—unless they own closely related breeding stock whose value would be enhanced by a star in the family. If he fails miserably, they'll cross the street to avoid you.

Buying privately does give you the rare advantage of bringing in a vet to kick the tires. Without his help, you'll get nowhere trying to barter objectively with someone who is selling you his pride and joy. A man's own horse is always worth twice the fair market value, while all other horses are dog meat in his eyes. You can easily hide behind the skirts of the vet's professional opinion in search of an excuse not to buy a mutt from a friend.

The seductive side of private buying is that you can engineer terms which will help compensate for the sticky emotionalism involved. For instance, buying a horse "on the cuff" means that you agree to pay for him out of his earnings. Another sweet deal to cook is a buy-back guarantee. If the horse does not earn a stipulated amount by a certain time, the seller will be obligated to buy him back at the original price. In both cases, the seller either has immense confidence in his horse or is in a seething hurry to get rid of him.

AUCTIONS

Auctions are more than just convenient arenas where you can buy and sell horses. They are a marketplace in the oldest and quaintest sense of the word. Every local breeder and owner of note is there. Fashion trends, not only in duck shoes and muck-out clothes, but in horse pedigree and type, are scrutinized and followed.

Some people don't care for bidding. Perhaps they're leery of the shenanigans of a foxy auctioneer or of consignors who bid up their own prices. Auctions can still be valuable, though, if only to give you a general feel for what livestock is selling for. Armed with this knowledge, you can be a shrewder customer when buying directly off the tracks and farms.

Go to a few. The auctioneer's yodeling has an eerie rhythm of its own, while the parade of highly polished horseflesh has a mesmerizing flow. Rouse yourself to break in the catalog well, run your eyes and hands over everything nice, and set limits on the horses you like.

Sometimes you'll set your cap on a particular horse to the extent of passing up earlier hip numbers—just what it sounds like, they stick the catalog number on the hip. If you get outbid, don't buy any old thing just to keep from going home empty-handed. Be cool. Great bargains can be found at the tail-end of a sale after the crowd has gotten sated and sleepy, and gone home. But these horses are real bargains only if they have not been bought back by their consignors who have the right to set a minimum release or "upset" price.

Suppose for a moment that you put in the highest final bid, but it fell short of the secret reserve price. The auctioneer would then sing out the code name for a ficticious bidder at the next higher increment. This way you'll at least know that you didn't get the horse, although nobody will really know why. It protects the sale's ambiance: you don't want bidders getting disheartened by too many buy-backs.

Start out small, buy a weanling. Weanlings are fun to get from the mixed sales each fall to give your homebreds a little competition and companionship. Some professionals go in for "pin-hooking" at this stage, which means buying young stock for resale later. But many think it's far too risky because it's so tough to predict how a weanling will look when fully grown. Bull. All youngsters—human and equine—have certain features and forms to their bodies that will stay with them all their lives. Class comes out in the way they carry themselves.

Because of a relatively low demand for weanlings, you can usually pick and choose and get just about anything you want. There will always be plenty of starving horsemen around who need to sell their weanling crop for ready cash, even though waiting for the yearling sales might be a better deal. The traditional rule of thumb is that weanlings should go for twice the sire's stud fee and that a yearling's fair price is four times the stud fee.

Buying weanlings is not only cheap, it's challenging. You'll be in a position to control all the special care, nutrition and schooling that goes into the next crucial growing years.

Come Prepared

Auction houses fret over the need to get buyers to establish credit at the cashier's office as their first order of business. Sales companies are always looking for prompt payment, particularly since the consignor is due his share of the take come what may. No house is on fire to finance slow payers.

If you seriously expect to buy stock at an auction, remember to take feed, hay and buckets along with you. Consignors wash their hands of horses the minute they've been sold, and you may not be able to line up a van ride home for your new purchase that same day. Auction houses promise to keep an eye on the sold animals for 24 hours, but this service is less than punctilious. Don't go begging here and there for the bare necessities; be a good boy scout.

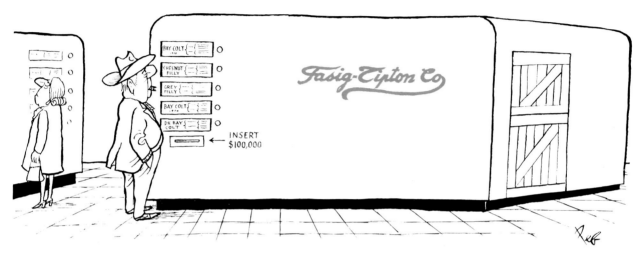

BAY COLT

CHESNUT
FILLY

GREY
FILLY

BAY COLT

DK BAY
COLT

INSERT
$100,000

Fasig-Tipton Co

ONLY DREAMS ARE FREE

The saga of Grimshaw began with the rap of a gavel knocking him down for 25 grand. From the start we broke all the rules, mainly our own. By-passed homework. Never even saw the horse run, the crux of any "Two-year-olds in Training" sale. Excuses don't help. He ran like a clod.

We were buoyed by friends and we played to the crowd. They wanted us to buy a horse, any one would do. Grimshaw was pretty and fashionably bred . . . the proverbial sugarplums danced overhead.

He never showed much as a runner, but still we babied our money along, kidding ourselves into believing everything we wanted to hear.

"All Quadrangle colts come to hand slowly."

What we didn't realize was that no brains trumped by a small heart can be as detrimental in horses as it is in humans. Possibly more so. Grimshaw's field-trailing first six starts were lost chances to make a buck.

Grimshaw bowed. When you see it coming, lose the horse. Bows are stretched and torn tendons which never seem to heal. It's like being a little bit pregnant.

"What he needs is a good long vacation."

Except that bows have a tendency of coming back. All went well until push came to shove. With the pressure of work, the tendon would sting; without work, the horse could not get fit.

One win and $40,000 poorer, we lost Grimshaw with a sigh of relief for $3500. Learn something—anything—from all this.

CLAIMING
Tactics

Although racing quickens the pulse at any level, there is an extra edge to claiming races which helps compensate for their lowly status. Psyching out the competition makes for an absorbing game. When you're ready to stake out a horse to claim, that game becomes as compelling as the primordial thrill of the hunt. It's risky. You can't feel legs or jog them for soundness. You must rely entirely on *RACING FORM* stats, general appearance and a heavy dose of instinct. Pinpointing a great claim is the easy part; it takes balls to lay your money down.

If you believe in laissez-faire trade and want to have a free hand in buying and selling racehorses, glare at your fellow owners and act your most inhospitable, boorish worst. Friendships are a dead weight. They turn into unspoken agreements not to claim horses off one another. Your stock will stagnate when claiming becomes an act of war.

There is no sure-fire way to ensure that every horse you claim will make money for you. Learn to be philosophical about lemons. How cavalierly you play the game depends on how easily you can absorb your losses.

RUNNING MACHINE

Running Machine made cowards of us all. His right knee was huge and ugly with lumps of calcium built far out to the front. But the sonofabitch could run. Demolished track records.

Ran in the cheapest races with no one around. Trainers swore and groused, but—dammit—couldn't bring themselves to fill out a claim. The track vet pulled his hat down low when Running Machine came hobbling back at picture time.

His winnings kept mounting. We knew it had to end; the question was when. The next race or ten more down the line.

Racing tests you. Sometimes all that teasing can get to you, so you go ahead and drop in a claim slip. Wouldn't you know, that'll be the day the horse comes home in a cart. It can be a brutal game of dare, to see who scares or who is too greedy to care.

©DAILY RACING FORM

Everybody has a pet claiming ploy. One of the nation's top trainers, in terms of races won, operates a huge and successful claiming stable for several owners with the keynote policy of claiming horses on the raise. He reasons that a horse who is being moved up the claiming ranks by being run in successively more expensive spots is a sound claim. The owner obviously has confidence in the horse's condition and ability, and is interested in protecting his investment by raising the claiming price.

Other trainers are less subtle in their thinking and would rather not pay a premium claiming price. What's more, trainers get cold feet about claiming high when they consider that the horse will have to be run at the next higher level for 30 more days. Other than this rule, horses are free to be moved up and down at the discretion of their connections to find the biggest purse in the easiest race.

Some iron-gutted horsemen look for a bargain claim in the form of a horse that has shown some talent in his past performances but is dropping down radically after a long vacation for what could be a nice win and confidence-builder. But there is a real danger here that the horse is being dropped because whatever precipitated his lay-off has not healed well enough. He could be worth zilch.

Yet another gambit that can pay off is claiming at the upper levels of each track. This is where most people feel safe in running a good horse. Claiming is always hot and heavy in the middle of the scale, though not at the top and usually not at the bottom. That's why if you have a winning horse of average ability, you cannot expect to hold onto him forever in the medium levels. You'd be safer shipping him to a smaller track where he could qualify to run with horses of the first circle. The top level at any track is rarely affordable for local interests.

There is great potential in claiming a horse that has been mismanaged or is in the hands of an incompetent trainer. It should be easy to improve his race record as long as he has not been ruined. You can also find some good pickings among the larger claiming outfits that are satisfied to drop a horse once he has paid for himself, provided he shows no signs of setting the world on fire. Smaller stables, on the other hand, are often desperate to hold onto any usable stock and tend to overprotect and run their horses at inflated values.

Strategy

Whatever your claiming tactics, the first order of business is to make a habit of scanning the *DAILY RACING FORM's* past performance section looking for interesting horses on every racing card. When something catches your eye in the *RACING FORM*, you must be organized and ready to make a final assessment as soon as the horse comes in for saddling. Time is of the essence. All claims must be submitted 15 minutes before post time. If a trainer is cagey and doesn't want to lose his horse, he'll be sure to wait until the last minute to enter the paddock, risking a minor fine for the privilege of being late.

Claiming doesn't let you feel a horse's legs, but you can usually spot the worst types of problems, like bows and joint injuries. That's why most trainers are afraid of a horse with four racing bandages. Although these bandages could be clever cover-ups, the feeling here is that they weigh too much to be put on as red herrings. Horses with them, need them.

If perfect racehorses are rare, perfect claims are even scarcer. But you might find that it's easier to work with a hard-knocking horse, even if he has some minor physical problems, than with a sound but spineless ne'er-do-well.

Decision. During the final seconds that you have to decide aye or nay on a claim, sum up your impressions of the horse. Would you be proud to own him? You are going to have to live with him, and you'll be reminded of that every month at bill-paying time.

Recognize the Look of Eagles.

—*Courtesy of THE BLOOD-HORSE.*

The FORM at a Glance . . .

6 **BOWIE**

6 FURLONGS. (1.08) CLAIMING. Purse $8,500. 3-year-olds and upward. Weights, 3-year-olds 115 lbs. Older 122 lbs. Non-winners of two races since June 10 allowed 3 lbs. A race 5 lbs. A race since June 3, 8 lbs. Claiming Price $35,000; for each $2,500 to $30,000, 1 lb. (Races where entered for $27,500 or less not considered.)

Century Rollick
Own.—Stevens Pauline

B. h. 6, by Rollicking—Rhombus, by Bold Effort
$30,000 **Br.—Century Breeders (Md)**
Tr.—Dillow John H

112

Lifetime								
55 9 13 7	**1983**	**14**	**5**	**4**	**2**	**$30,700**
$88,514	**1982**	**7**	**0**	**0**	**1**	**$1,380**
	Turf	**3**	**0**	**0**	**0**	

2Jly83- 2Bow	fst	6f	:22	:45⅖	1:11⅕	Clm 18500	8	6	6^{12}	6^{12}	$4^{4½}$	1^{nk}	Hinojosa H	b	114	3.90	84-21	Century Rollick 114^{nk} Sailing Light 115^{1}Flatter$117^{1¼}$	Wide, drvng	8
21Jun83- 7Bow	gd	6f	:22⅘	:46	1:11⅘	Clm 13500	3	3	1½	1^{hd}	1½	1^{1}	Delgado A	b	112	2.40	81-30	Century Rollick 112^{1} VicTheBrute$114^{3½}$OurFirstTime115^{6}	Driving	7
11Jun83- 4Pim	fst	6f	:23⅖	:47	1:11⅖	Clm c-8500	5	2	3^{1}	2^{hd}	1^{hd}	1^{4}	Byrnes D	b	119	*1.50	89-18	Century Rollick 119^{4} He'sTerrific$114^{4¼}$JoveInMotion114^{1}	Driving	8
2Jun83- 2Pim	fst	6f	:23⅗	:46⅘	1:11⅘	Clm 8500	5	3	$4^{2½}$	$2^{1½}$	1^{hd}	1^{4}	Byrnes D	b	114	3.30	87-19	Century Rollick114^{4}FetaCheese$114^{2½}$SpringInAthens114^{2}	Drew of	7
27May83- 6Pim	fst	6f	:23⅖	:46⅕	1:11⅕	Clm 18500	2	2	$4^{4½}$	6^{12}	6^{17}	6^{25}	Miller D A Jr	b	114	2.10	65-22	Guy $119^{4½}$ Featured Star $108^{1¾}$ Northern Barbizon$114^{3¾}$	Ret. sore	6
6May83- 6Pim	fst	6f	:23⅕	:46⅖	1:11⅘	Clm 18500	5	2	$3^{1½}$	$3^{1½}$	2^{1}	2^{nk}	Krone J A	b	114	6.90	87-22	Cha Cha Pop 109^{nk} Century Rollick 114^{3} FeaturedStar112^{4}	Hung	7
22Apr83- 3Aqu	fst	6f	:22⅗	:45⅗	1:10⅗	Clm 16000	7	2	5^{4}	5^{5}	4^{2}	$3^{2¾}$	Messina R^{5}	b	112	14.40	85-16	Colonel Law $117^{1¾}$Rapido'sRepeat117^{1}CenturyRollick$112^{¾}$	Rallied	9
25Mar83- 6Pim	fst	6f	:23⅖	:48⅕	1:13	Clm 18500	7	5	$6^{2¼}$	2^{hd}	$4^{1½}$	5^{4}	Wright D R	b	119	10.90	77-27	Featured Star $109^{¾}$ Jara 115^{nk} Bright Talisman 115^{1}	Wide, str.	8
15Mar83- 5Bow	fst	7f	:23⅗	:46⅘	1:24	Clm 18500	4	3	3^{1}	3^{2}	3^{2}	$3^{4½}$	Kaenel J L	b	119	4.30	80-25	Super Judge $109^{1½}$ Beirut II 117^{3} CenturyRollick$119^{2½}$	Weakened	6
5Mar83- 3Bow	fst	6f	:23	:46⅘	1:11⅘	Clm 18500	7	3	$3^{1½}$	$3^{1½}$	2^{hd}	1^{1}	Miller D A Jr	b	114	*1.70	81-23	CenturyRollick114^{1}BrightTalisman114^{3}BltimoreBlde114^{no}	Driving	8

LATEST WORKOUTS May 25 Lrl 4f gd :49⅗ b May 21 Lrl 4f fst :53⅕ b

Century Rollick seems to be a very talented horse with some serious physical problems. These must have kept him from doing much of anything in 1982, although previous to that he had won over $50,000. In 1983, he was badly beaten only once—sixth by 25 lengths on May 27. This debacle and the remark, "Returned sore," sufficed to keep the buyers away when he was dropped in at $8500. Running him back again at that same level after he had won there served to reinforce the notion that time was running out for his racing career.

It probably still is, but the stout-hearted folks who claimed him got lucky: the horse shows a renewed appetite for winning and obviously doesn't hurt while he's running. Century Rollick's a dream claim in terms of winnings. Most owners and trainers, though, wouldn't relish the anxiety of wondering how long he'll hold up. This thought doesn't seem to bother his connections. They're on one hell of a roll, moving him up the ladder win after win, going after those big purses.

How to Milk the RACING FORM

Claiming a horse is like buying a sports coat. Know what you want, but keep an open mind. If you insist on day-glo stripes, you might just go home empty-handed.

Shopping's fun but it ain't easy. Expect to spend an hour a day hunched over the *RACING FORM*. It will become one of life's real pleasures. When you're ready to spend, don't just give your agent the nod. Be there in person and visually try the horse on.

Looking for somewhere to start, go through and circle the favorites mentioned in the *FORM's* consensus. Most claimable horses are the favorites—they are placed right, worth the money. With this in mind, drop in your claim slip as late as allowable so that you can keep an eye on the toteboard. If a horse is dead cold on the board, then his connections don't even think enough of him to make a good bet.

Step by Step

Pedigree. You can virtually ignore the pedigree print-out unless you've got one eye on the stud barn. Among the racing ranks, a good pedigree doesn't hold for much unless you do it proud. That's why you can sometimes buy a well-bred broodmare or stallion prospect at wholesale prices on the track.

Management. Homebreds are usually mismanaged, that is, over-protected for sentimental reasons. So whenever you see the same name listed under owner and breeder, you can safely assume the horse really isn't much if they're running him cheap. If the owner and trainer are the same guy, though, the motives are harder to gauge. Trainers are wily by profession.

If the trainer is lousy, he'll usually employ a lousy jockey, so his horse may be struggling along with two strikes against him. This horse has good potential to show his gratitude for having been claimed by jumping up and winning for you.

Racing Level. You can't go far without checking out the price, distance and conditions of each race to see how it fits within the framework of your claiming needs. Note whether the horse is ascending or plummeting down the claim race ladder. Where he's been finishing on each level, close up or U.T., will clue you in on the line of thought in management. If on the drop, do they want to lose him or do they just want to win?

It's easy enough to go on from there to figure out how many lengths he was beaten by each time he missed out and, equally important, who beat him. This last is called the "company line." It's no humiliation to be beaten by a winner of stature.

Earnings. A horse's win/loss record and lifetime earnings may be a superficial measurement, but if you play the percentages it will give you a pretty good idea about a horse's winning attitude.

Turnover & Age. With older horses, you can gauge their degree of desirability by how many times they've been claimed. With the younger ones, make up your own rules. Two–year–olds (2yos) are often overpriced as their optimistic owners sit by patiently waiting for these horses to grow into themselves. Three–year–olds (3yos) are interesting at the beginning of the year, heading into a long season of "3yos only" races. It's grand if you can find a 3yo that likes to go long because there are not too many good distance horses at that age and you stand to make some money with him. Still, you'd rarely want to claim a 3yo running right on the bottom—this is the sweet season and things won't get any easier for him.

Once a horse reaches four, age doesn't get much emphasis. Any age up to nine is fine.

Patterns. Check the race dates to see how frequently a horse has run. If the dates are far apart, suspect chronic injuries. It's hard to make money with a horse that can only hold together for a handful of races a year.

It's time to address yourself to the grid of figures. You're looking for a certain consistency which points up the horse's running style. Sucker horses (perennially second) are intriguing especially if they were beaten favorites. Every trainer feels he can add that certain something to turn this kind of horse into a winner. As it is, the horse is still a money–maker.

If you have access to speed figures, use them to boil down a horse's running potential. Otherwise, couple your imagination with the handy speed ratings and track variants served up by the *RACING FORM.* (See Appendix.) You can make allowances for poor showings by 2yos and 3yos, especially the fillies, but by the time a horse hits four he should have developed his running potential enough to cut a nice figure.

Sometimes a horse that has won two or three in a row is not the perfect claim. First, you'll wonder why he is still in the affordable ranks with that kind of track record. And second, the law of averages says that he's peaked.

Sign Posts. Too many fast workouts might mean that a horse is hanging out a great big "for sale" sign. No new workouts at all could make you suspicious that a horse may not be able to take the physical strain of hard exercise between races. But it's a foggy area. Some horses just don't need that additional work.

Horses that ship in are worth a passing glance. Try to get at the motive behind the shipping. It could be a question of having no place else to run. Or, the connections could be trying to dump a dunce on horsemen who don't know about that horse's follies.

Where Can You Go From Here? You've always got to consider whether a claiming prospect can handle the next step up. It may not only be a dollar jump but a strongly delineated leap in class. Claiming races come in bunches at the low, medium and high levels. For example, $11,500 and $14,500 may be virtually interchangeable with horses entered indiscriminately depending on which race the Racing Secretary happens to card. But $18,500 is another story with significantly more talented horses running at that level. It's a big psychological barrier.

Good management of a claimed horse can ease the way to better racing results. Unsophisticated trainers will unfairly pit girls against boys, 3yos against older horses and maidens against winners. Besides spotting a horse more sensibly, a couple of other tricks put into play by a new trainer can make the crucial difference. Young horses may need blinkers to focus on racing; bleeder horses may need Lasix to breathe free and run.

It's nice to claim a horse with lots of options open to him. The easiest races to win are "maiden" races for non-winners, but you would never want to claim an inveterate maiden. Look for one with a few starts who has been close up at the finish. Major tracks usually don't go on to card "non-winners of two (or three) races" except as allowance race conditions. Too bad. These are sweet and easy conditions to run through at the small tracks.

While searching for a horse with plenty of conditions open to him, you might check out candidates for starter allowance or handicap races. To qualify for these, a horse must have run in a relatively cheap level at some time within the year. A talented horse might get away with running cheap because of a lay-off, old age or a temporary slump. At any rate, qualifying for starter races may open up great new opportunities, although it's always a big gamble to claim a horse who's been on the bottom.

Treat the *RACING FORM* like a purebred Guernsey milker. If you stroke her like you should, you'll have a rich barn full of heart-warming success stories. Prolong your fun and claim just one horse at a time. The best claims habitually come haunting long after you've spent your last dime.

Evaluate the Claim.

Health. The first thing most trainers do with an expensive new claim is have the vet take a reading on him with a barrage of medical tests. A comprehensive blood test is expensive but horsemen feel that it can show up immediately correctable problems like a low blood count, a high level of worms and abnormalities in enzymes which might indicate poor condition. A simple fecal count is also thought to do the trick for analyzing the worm situation and is routinely done for cheaper claims.

Some vets consider both blood counts and fecal counts as ham-handed measurements whose results could be swayed by any number of irrelevant conditions. The fact remains, though, that enriching the blood and controlling the worm population can lead to an immediate improvement in performance.

Newly claimed horses are routinely given the jug, which is a transfusion of electrolytes to help them over their post-race stress, and to help the jug-makers over any financial worries. Sometimes trainers feel that hormones are called for to stimulate the adrenal system and tighten up the joints, even though they're playing with fire.

Pumped full of wormers, tonics, medicine or whatever, the new claim is then put on a regimen of excellent feed and hay and the popular supplement of the day. Horses take on the sheen of good care from one day to the next. Given an extra dose of TLC, nervous types can easily start to exude confidence.

All this blooming health won't get you too far if a horse's wheels can't roll across the finish line. Don't be a piker, go ahead and order a complete set of knee and ankle x-rays so that you know right off what you've got to work with in those critical areas.

Injuries. Trainers like to go easy with a new claim until they get a good feel for him. Every horse is given a couple of days off anyway after a race to relax before going back into training. This is important because bone density actually decreases with racing stress. You've got to give a working racehorse enough shore leave to let his bones remineralize. (See Chapter Seven.)

The newly claimed horse initially spends his half hour exercise period walking the shedrow under the trainer's searching eye. It may take a while for the post-race kinks to rise to the surface and make him feel a little off, sore, lame or crippled.

Science is invading the shedrow and it beats hocus-pocus for diagnostic precision. Common joint injuries have been traditionally treated with an unbelievably heavy hand, a literal shot in the dark. There is now a diagnostic service which takes you a step beyond peering into fuzzy x-rays. It can examine a small amount of joint fluid and tell you exactly what stage of deterioration a joint is in. While x-rays only point up bone chips, cracks or growths, this service measures the degree of intra-articular inflammation. By analyzing the amount of protein impurities in the synovial fluid and any decrease in its viscosity, they can not only grade the problem, but recommend a precise course of treatment.

In young horses, joint problems are usually just inflammation of the joint capsule, a pull and tear situation. This is where tapping can do the most good. Tapping entails drawing out excess fluid and blood, then injecting cortisone (anti-inflammatory) and possibly some hyaluronic acid (lubricating). Then you might want to rest the horse for a while or start swimming him. If you can afford it.

STUCK

Beautifully bred and in for a song after a long lay-off, Flying Sugar looked like a textbook case of how to steal a race. They say that God hates a coward and, believe me, He must have loved us that day.

I guess Flying Sugar ran a couple of steps, but he wasn't long in pulling up. We howled and fumed as the horse ambulance drove out to bring home our new claim.

"Sorry folks, the claim slip jammed in the machine. We had to nullify your claim and another guy got the horse."

To win you must lose. It happens.

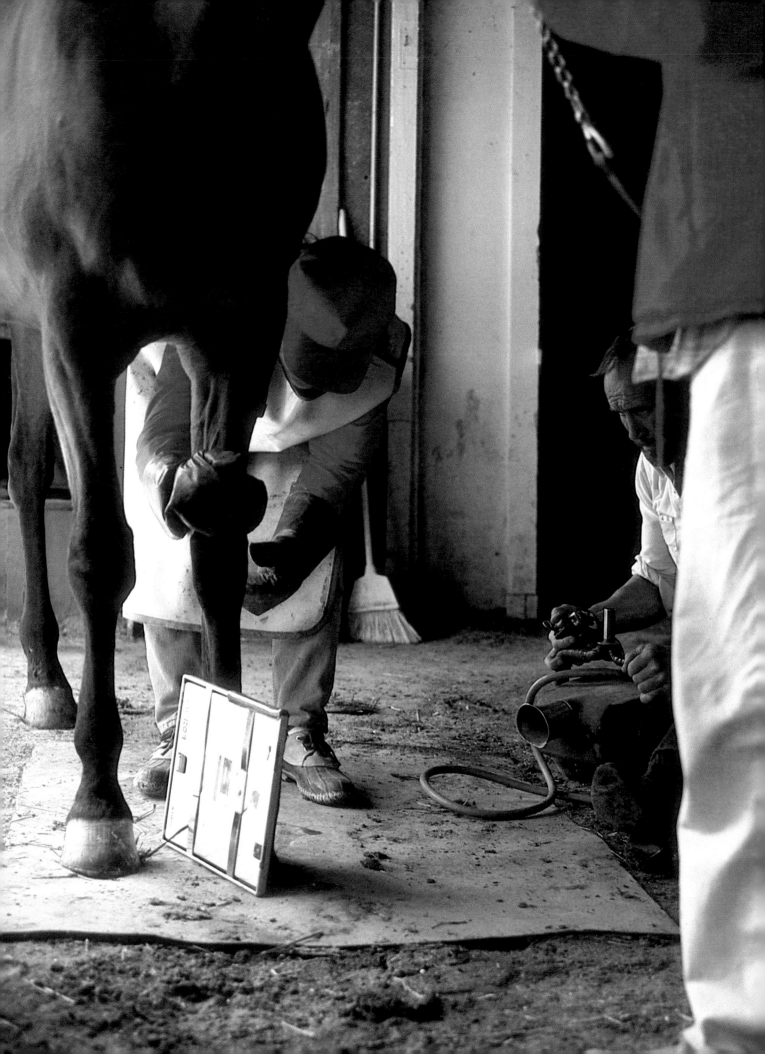

Older horses can have tougher problems resulting from the erosion of the joint surfaces. Chips and spurs (calcium deposits) occur in the boney area. Something like hyaluronic acid might stand a crack at oiling these joints and relieving the pain. There's also surgery and a handful of other tricks, but nothing's a sure cure for wear and tear. Maybe a leg transplant.

Given time off, the lower joints of an animal will sometimes grow calcified or "set." Ankles may become huge and flexion nil, yet as long as they stay cold they won't bother the horse much at all.

©DAILY RACING FORM

The irony of injures is that the horse with the most heart gets hurt first. He's too aggressive to heed his body's warning signs. Some trainers beg for sound horses. Others know that the one with four bandages can beat the wimps, live with the pain and be ready to run again.

Game Plan. Hopefully the right medication, diet, care and exercise will make it easy to step a claimed horse into the next higher level. The lukewarm claim that needs more time to recuperate or shows little potential can wait the required 30 days and go back into the races at the same level. He has done his time and is out of jail. Only a few madmen would be tempted to reclaim a horse at this original level since the first thought to pop into mind is that something must be radically wrong with the horse. The reasoning is that few owners would be willing to take a chance on losing a promising horse with so little profit. Or would they? Trackmen excel in double-think.

Whenever you have an inkling that a claim might develop into something nice, take a moment to order a sales catalog type of pedigree from your local Thoroughbred association or bloodstock agency. All you need to give is the name and date of birth, and you can usually get a read-out within a couple of days of your phone call. Pedigrees are revealing. They might show up a family proclivity for turf racing or for going distance of ground. Extra information cuts back on guesswork.

Unfortunately, the same way that big betting wins can work out to be no more than loans from the track to keep you pushing money through the window, the spectacularly bad claims you make have a nasty way of cancelling out the good ones when you go in for high-risk claiming gambles. Don't dwell on reverses. One day you will find that special horse who will make up for all the indignities, large and small.

Tailoring a Training Regime

Sportsmedicine. The new Sportsmedicine approach is urging progressive trainers to come up with more creative training schedules, specifically addressed to the needs of each individual animal. Technology and a scientific frame of mind can help a trainer to evaluate a horse's condition in terms of soundness, fitness and talent. Ultrasound diagnosis of lameness, cinematography, measuring heartbeat and analyzing muscle fiber are all at the tip of an emerging iceberg. The results of these tests could tell the trainer whether a horse needs endurance or speed work, and how much he can handle. (See Chapter Six.)

Training may become more complicated in the short term, but better in the long. Training bills will likewise soar, but remember that the biggest expense of all is a broken-down racehorse. The biggest heartbreak, too.

'HORSE NUMBER TWO PRESENTS EXCITING CHROMOSOME ABNORMALITIES !'

Trackwork. At the moment, only very sore or very talented horses are trained with any great deliberation. A run-of-the-mill claimed horse is usually racing fit so that standard training would begin by jogging him the wrong way around the track—it's easier to control and slow horses down going in the wrong direction. The next day, your plater might be sent out to gallop a mile or so around the track. A few days later, he could be pressed to put in an invigorating "two-minute lick," which is one mile run in two minutes. This horse will probably be "blown out" in a short, fast sprint a couple of days before racing, although there are some horsemen who think that "works" or timed all-out gallops are unnecessary as long as a horse is being sent out to run every couple of weeks.

On the Farm. Most know-it-alls agree that training a horse on a track is the best way to keep a sound horse race-worthy. But a horse that looks to be getting a little sour (23 hours a day in the same stall gets to be a drag year-in, year-out) can sometimes benefit from a working holiday in the paddocks of a nearby farm. As long as he is doing some running around in the fresh air each day training himself, he might be able to work out his soreness while staying in racing shape. He'll lose his edge, though, unless he continues to race regularly.

In the Pool. Every horse can swim, although some need convincing the first time in. Just as running talent differs, swimmers are entirely different in style, smoothness and speed. But the initial plunge—no matter how brief—can be counted on to reduce every horse to quivering exhaustion.

Most swimmers will also need some track work on the side to get competitively fit and fast, unless they are running in company far below their natural level. This is not to downgrade the exertions of swimming. Although submaximal exercise, horses have been thought to suffer heart attacks from being prodded too far, too soon.

Swimming is a great half-way measure between frolicking on the farm and training in earnest at the track. Concussion injuries, like questionable ankles and knees, will particularly benefit from use of the pool; in fact, it's about the best therapy during the recovery stage of any injury. But, let's face it, the horse that needs swimming on a regular, on-going basis in order to stay in the game might well be on racing's death row.

MARK SPITZ

Tanqueray had an ankle which called for the cure of the day. A mercury blister was applied to stimulate circulation and healing, though most vets will agree the real healer is rest. After a few months off, Tanqueray was shipped to a swim spa as a smooth way of easing into the jarring routine of racing.

When the year rolled into winter, we began to balk at the thought of sending her back to the ice-hardened track. Tanqueray swam the Atlantic and the Pacific and parts of the Indian Ocean, while winter dragged on frozen and long.

Spring. Tanqueray came back her valiant self, only she ran kind of funny. Her nose was shot skyward, sucking in air with an olympic swimmer's stance.

The Bitter End

Just as making a good claim can give you a rush of Christmas Eve, having a nice horse claimed from you can tarnish the glow off any victory. The only way to handle this feeling is to steel yourself with the remembrance that horseracing is, after all, a business. There's no point in breast-beating or in starting a vendetta against another trainer for buying your horse. Whenever you enter a horse in a claiming race with your eye on the purse of an easy win, you have de facto acknowledged that your horse is for sale. If you're scared to death of losing a claiming level horse, take him home and leave him in your backyard.

Sooner or later, you'll realize just how much you need to have horses claimed off you for a healthy turnover in stock. Chances are that other horsemen will relieve you of a good many bums in the long run. Sometimes netting a decent final sale price makes the difference between showing an overall profit instead of a loss on an unimposing animal.

Your ego might get bruised occasionally if someone goes on to do much better with your horse than you did, but on the whole, only a true misanthrope would begrudge any horse his day in the sun. All horses go off form sooner or later, so be content not to drink the cup down to the last drop.

Animal-lovers might have trouble with the next consideration but it would be less than fair not to show racing's brutal side. Although it's a far cry from rough contact sports like football, racing brings with it injuries, and some are serious enough to preclude a comfortable and useful life, even at stud.

If you can find someone with a kind heart and pastures to spare, you might give the retirement angle a whirl. Along these lines, plans and an all-star Board of Directors have been drawn up for a Golden Years home in New York state. Even though prison labor is to be used in a mutually therapeutic way, costs are bound to be high and the amount of horses accepted severely limited. The idea may be quixotic, but it is nice.

Once you've exhausted the gift-horse option (it can be tax-free to a school or charity), often the only humane choice left is to put the animal out of its suffering. This is euphemistically called sending a horse "down the road" with the understanding that the end of the road is an auction where horseflesh is bought by the pound. To carry the grisly metaphor even further, the owner who ends up with a washed-up horse of no racing value is said to "eat the horse." Horses continue to serve others well even if fate calls for them to end up recycled on a dinner plate or doggy bowl.

DYING TO RUN

Don's Double was a hard-knocking little racehorse who was taking his first plunge into the shark-filled waters of the lower claiming ranks. We lurked there blood-crazed, ready to pounce.

Once in a blue moon there is more than one claim put in for a horse, which calls for a "shake." The sight of seven other claiming interests gathered in the Secretary's Office never dented our confidence. We won the drawing and tried to ignore the grim looks of envy being cast our way.

The others should have known. Nothing is that easy. Nobody is too lucky.

A few weeks later we put an entry into a race. We won it with one horse, but lost the other. Don's Double ended up in a heap coming into the stretch. The irony and the agony say it all.

⟨) Chapter Six (⟩

TRACKBOUND

LAY OF THE LAND

Each U.S. racetrack has its own special characteristics—size, angle of turns, length of straightaway—but they are all oval and in no way as disparate as the venerable and oddly shaped courses that can be found in England and on the continent. The big trackside structures house a grandstand and a clubhouse. The clubhouse is supposed to be a shade more elegant, and contains the quality restaurants. Tracks no longer have special accommodations for owners—they are now considered "jes' folks," if only a little crazier than everyone else.

Races must be planned so that the finish line is always in front of the main plant. A starting gate is set on wheels so that it can be pulled from spot to spot and set at various distances from the finish line, depending on the length of the race. A mile race on a mile track would naturally start just about at the finish line. Horses race counter-clockwise from the start: the field would move first into the clubhouse turn, then down the backside, into the far turn and up the stretch.

Color-coded poles and markers denote distances from the finish line all the way around. The most often cited are the striped poles in the homestretch. If the result chart write-up in the *RACING FORM* says that your horse got overtaken at the quarter pole, but came back at the sixteenth to win drawing away, you'll know then that he was in trouble a quarter of a mile from the finish line, but fought his way to the front a sixteenth of a mile from home.

Tracks can become known by the famous voices of their callers. These pros pull it all together and bring their personal flair to racing. They've learned to block out the world minutes before each race and concentrate totally on absorbing the names and colors of the next starters. But good delivery is the toughest part. It's calculated to send shivers down your spine whenever your horse gets called on top.

The caller is helped along by patrol judges stationed all around the track who keep an eye on the race's progress. If something looks bad, they'll recommend that the stewards call for an inquiry and review the race tapes from all angles. The stewards will also examine the tapes if a jockey objects to the race results on the grounds that he was illegally impeded. An ill-considered objection can bring a fine down on a jock's head to cut short any fishing expeditions. Even so, all eyes stay riveted on the incoming jockeys after every race to see which ones will head for the phone to lodge a complaint. No one breathes easily until these jocks are safely in their underwear.

You can buy video tapes of your favorite races from the TV cameraman. The personality of each cameraman determines how elaborately the tapes will be run off for you. Race tapes can include the post parade, the race shot from several different camera angles (along with a running commentary from the patrol judges), and hopefully your triumphant entry into the winner's circle. Most cameramen are anxious to oblige your every wish. Selling tapes is a source of quick and easy money.

The Mile Track

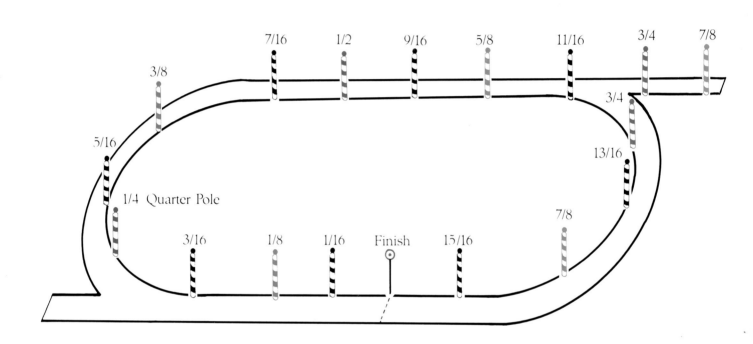

Quarter Pole—red & white
Eighth Pole—green & white
Sixteenth Pole—black & white

OK, LET ME GET IT STRAIGHT NOW: TAKE HIM TO THE FRONT, EASE BACK ON THE TURN, SETTLE HIM INTO 4TH ON THE...

...BACKSTRETCH, MOVE AROUND HORSES ON THE TURN, CUT TO THE INSIDE COMING INTO THE STRETCH, HIT HIM 3 TIMES LEFT HANDED AND 4 TIMES RIGHT HANDED...

... OR IS IT 4 TIMES LEFT HANDED AND 3 TIMES RIGHT HANDED?

Watching tapes is also a source of quick and easy owner gratification. You can prolong your happiness indefinitely by replaying hours of winning efforts. The best part is the assurance of a happy ending.

POWER CELLS
Racing Secretary's Office

The People. The Secretary's Office is the center of the horseman's world. The noise level can get as high as any city newsroom, but there the comparison ends. These people are controlling the life of the track, not just recording it.

The Racing Secretary is supported by a talented staff that makes this world go 'round. They have the most sought-after jobs on the track. They're the patrol judges, they man the phones, shuffle papers and stave off petitioning horsemen.

If you watch closely, you'll see there's a team. These guys are dedicated. They have to be—their day begins early. They'll basically stay together on a circuit, moving from meet to meet. Every once in a while, an outstanding player will be asked to move up to a prestigious job on another circuit.

The Racing Secretary is the pacesetter. Each has a tact of his own for weighing the wishes of the bettors against the needs of the horsemen. The best are approachable, sensitive and diplomatic. But they can be irresistible negotiators. Nobody forgets that behind the charm lies the undisputed power of an Oriental Pasha.

The Job. If the Racing Secretary is enterprising, he can manage the show with an impresario's touch. A few minutes added here and there, with a longer post parade and later post time, can turn into an appreciable profit at the betting windows. A Racing Secretary is not accountable for the handle, but his pride is bound up with the success of the meet.

Taking Entries. Keeping an eye on the money figures is one way to find out which races are most popular with the betting man. The figs always prove that higher class horses draw in the spending fans. But these races are difficult to card, and it helps to have a file on the local allowance horses to see who is ready to run and under what conditions. Otherwise, drawing a short field means risking financial disaster if a couple of horses post late scratches.

Tracks vary on their deadlines for entering but it is always a couple of days before an "overnight race." Post positions are decided by using billiard pills. This way it's blind and impartial.

Each track has rules printed in the condition book on the minimum number of horses needed for a race to "fill." Scratches can be made without penalty before a certain time if a large enough field is drawn. In a short field, you're stuck unless you can produce a vet's certificate. Even then, you're usually not supposed to re-enter your horse in another race for five more days. If you are pig-headed enough to enter anyway at a different track, anyone at all (usually the connections of the horse you beat) can blow the whistle on you and make you forfeit the purse.

Nominations for most stakes races are taken two weeks before the event. A few big stakes races will involve a series of nominating fees which have to be made starting months beforehand, sometimes when the prospective runner is still in utero. Either way, the attrition rate of the original nominees is so high that most stakes—with the notable exception of the Kentucky Derby—allow for supplemental nominations at plush prices. All fees go into the pot, making the stakes considerably sweeter and giving rise to one interpretation of why stakes races are called "added-money events." With the help of a generous sponsor, tracks will sometimes go out on a limb and advertise a large "guaranteed" pot.

SPAGHETTI POWER

The kid was incorrigible. He'd sneak over the fence and into the track. Just to hang around, bet some, raise a little hell.

As he grew older, you could see that Lou Raffetto had it all: brains and looks, money and family. But he couldn't keep away from the track. When they sent him off to a fancy school, he went out between classes and bought himself a racehorse. He trained, and the horse won.

Nobody hassled him much at home but they knew his worth and hoped he'd go on. Become a big-time lawyer. Instead, Lou went back to the track. Worked in the mail room, parked cars, drove the patrol judges, you name it.

In the right spot at the right time, he was too bright not to like. Made a name for himself, for his style, and horsemen approached him with assurance and respect. Lawyers come a dime a dozen, but a good Racing Secretary . . . now there's a man.

'UNLEADED ONLY!'

Assigning Weights. Imposts are fairly automatic in the claiming ranks and are set out clearly in the condition book. Win a race and gain a couple of pounds. If you ride a bug–boy, you can cut back down on the weight. Female and younger horses generally get a break.

Some railbirds will swear weight doesn't count in a sprint, but don't bet on it.

Handicap and stakes races today are basically the same thing. Originally, the Racing Secretary assigned the weight for a handicap to equalize talent regardless of age and sex. A true stakes race was organized more along the lines of an allowance race with weights assigned according to a formula set out in the conditions. But that distinction is splitting hairs, and the Racing Secretary regularly has the last word regardless of the event's title.

The Racing Secretary and his assistant also come up with the subjective assignments of weight for starter handicaps. A starter handicap is a hybrid race restricted to horses who happen to have started within the year at a certain low claiming price, but are rarely slouches. With their checkered histories, they need the Racing Secretary's expertise to weigh their relative values. Theoretically speaking, any perfectly handicapped race would result in a dead heat of all the starters.

General Business. Horsemen routinely stop by the Secretary's Office to catch up on scuttlebutt, drop in claim or entry slips and hound the Horsemen's Bookkeeper. In an adjoining cubbyhole, a representative from the Racing Commission stands ready to take care of any licensing problems. The Horsemen's Benevolent & Protective Association (HBPA) also maintains an outpost in the vicinity which stocks the condition books for the general geographic area.

Horsemen's Benevolent & Protective Association.

The HBPA has developed into the Arnold Schwarzenegger of the racing world. For years it has been the lonely but only unified voice of the horsemen. A vast, amorphous organization, it is now comprised of over 25 state and regional divisions, with one national office. In effect, the HBPA represents the majority of all Thoroughbred owners and trainers, and it knows its strength.

Taking care of the down–and–outers of the backstretch has always been HBPA's burden to shoulder. When owners began to qualify as racing's lost lambs, HBPA rolled up its sleeves and got to work as a lobbying unit for better purses and fairer treatment. Remember this and consider the purse percentages or lead pony fees which disappear into HBPA's pocket as money well spent.

Jockeys

Business. A smart jockey has an agent. Agents are expensive, they live off a percentage of the jockey's earnings. But the best are supersalesmen who can cover a lot more ground than just one jockey looking out for himself. Drumming up business, insinuating himself into the life of each stable and taking care of his boy, it's all a part of an agent's day.

JOCKEYS' AGENTS

©*DAILY RACING FORM*

Agents have great leeway to pick and choose the best mounts. A jock going it alone can't help but antagonize his customers any time he has to decide between horses. It becomes a personal judgment full of hurt feelings and repercussions, whereas everybody accepts an agent's coin toss as the usual tough business decision.

Spills. Jockeys are in a dangerous profession. The older ones know it. They try to ride the thin line between being aggressive and being foolhardy. The younger guys don't care. It's life in the fast lane.

Awareness of danger can lead to problems when horses are running in cheap claiming races. The top jockeys might be afraid to ride a horse "on the drop," especially if they've never ridden that horse before. They'll figure he's hurting. To forestall this problem, give the mount to an apprentice jockey who will be hungry enough to appreciate any chance to ride. Naming a bug-boy will also scare off claiming interests since it reinforces the halfway-true picture that no one else wanted to ride the horse.

Even trainers with excellent reputations—not butchers who send out lame horses—manage to get their unfair share of broken legs in the rough and tumble of it all. After a serious accident, you can be sure that the superstitious jockey community will become extremely leery of every horse in that stable. They'll ride with infuriating, if understandable, tentativeness. What's more, a stable that's built around one particular jockey's special riding style is in double trouble if that jockey gets hurt, or even if he just gets "days." A week or so of suspension is the stewards' way of spanking.

Weather. What people forget to give jockeys credit for is the bravery involved in riding against the elements now that year-round racing is routine. Even a rainstorm can be rough. Jockeys have to stack on some five pairs of clear goggles and push each pair down as soon as it gets mud-blinded. It's done in an action so deft you'll never see it happen.

Nothing gets to a jock as much as the bone-chilling cold. Any lightweight fashion goes, preferably ladies' pantyhose and surgeons' gloves. The wind-chill temperature on a racing horse can numb hands and cause the reins to slip loose unnoticed.

While it might take a force majeure before the track decides to cancel a card, jockey guild representatives have the power to close down the show at any time. But since jocks are paid to take chances, and the money is good, racing's party can be expected to go on rain, snow, wind or cold. The patrons stay warm and cheery.

As for the horses, most love the cold—makes 'em feel alive—and track records are broken with abandon on frozen-hard tracks. Ice pellets in the eyes are never much fun but neither is dirt, and both can be equally blinding. Racing is not for weaklings, human or equine.

Pride. Jockeys are the prima donnas of any track. They generally make more money than anyone else on the track—up to 10% of the winner's purse without any of the big expenses of owning or training horses—and probably more money than anybody has ever made in their entire family line. They parade before the public in their splendid silks. They are as exasperating and as essential as the horse himself. And there will be times when you will be awestruck by the beauty of a great and courageous ride.

'HERE COMES OUR JOCKEY NOW, BARBARA.'

138

Jock Talk

Race Instructions. There is a special talent in learning to talk to the jockey, how to say the right words that will ring the right bells. You should instill him with confidence, but don't make him complacent. Never ever tell your jockey that any race is a piece of cake. And when you want to explain away an obvious irregularity or injury so that he won't be scared, try not to confuse him with details. Communication becomes easier the longer you've known the jock, can tell what he's thinking and see what he needs. He's like your wife.

Jock talk is peculiar and succinct. Since the racetrack is traditionally a haven for those too restless for school, expressions have been honed over the years that get to the point without taxing the intellect:

"Come out shooting ducks"	Gun him from the start.
"Take the lead" *"Run with the lead"* *"Hook the lead"*	What it sounds like.
"Wrap up on him" *"Fold up"* *"Keep him under a hold"* *"Take a nine to five"*	Rate the horse. Ride high, let him relax and save his strength for a big run at the end.
"Save ground"	Go to the rail even if you are behind other horses.
"Don't run into a hole"	Don't get surrounded by horses. To get free or keep out of trouble, you might have to check the horse and lose momentum.
"Take him wide"	Go around other horses on the outside.
"Ask him"	Let the reins out a notch, cluck or chirp, "scrub" with your hands, use the whip . . . whatever works.
"Don't use him early" *"Make one run"*	Save it till the end.

Golden Oldies. After a race, anyone can get tired of hearing the same old shopworn excuses. Maybe it would help if the stock answers were printed up on a checklist. Just as some jocks don't pay much attention to instructions before the race, you wouldn't have to waste as much time listening to the old familiar stories afterward. Your jockey could just sing out a number in his haste to dismount.

#1 *"Uh . . . I think she* wants to go long."*

> Translation: This horse is so slow he should have no problem rambling on for miles.

#2 *"Seemed like the horse couldn't handle the track."*

> Translation: I didn't feel like exerting myself. I got bigger races coming up.

#3 *"She'll be tough next time."*

> Translation: The horse needed the race to get fit and put a little experience under his belt.
> or
> I'm not planning to pull your horse again.

*You'll hear most jockeys calling horses "she," indicating that they are as flighty and temperamental as the proverbial stereotype.

141

THE BACKSTRETCH

Men of All Work

The backstretch has a fence around it. People used to think that it was put there to keep out the undesirables. Now others say it was built to keep the madmen in. There are horsemen in the backstretch who have run almost as much as their horses. And they are still running—from bill collectors, wives and empty lives.

Home for many is above the shop. To say it's spartan is dressing it up. There's a "kitchen" for backside dining—edible and cheap—on a schedule catering to the morning crowd. Not much to do at night, even if you had some loose change in your pocket: few tracks locate near the hot spots. But sometimes there are pretty pony girls or, failing that, the horses to play with.

Because it doesn't coddle its workers, the track has an unusually open job market to get started in. Get licensed, then go talk to the gatehouse guard; he'll know who's short on help. You'll be sent along as a hotwalker—no glamor there, but any kid with alacrity can talk himself into a leg-up on a horse or something to rub. Firing is no big deal either. You just move on over to the next barn. A horse might be worth a hundred grand, but human flesh comes cheap, except when you stop to think about how much damage unskilled help can wreak.

New jocks are also given every chance to prove themselves. The apprentice allowance is five to 10 pounds calculated on a complicated formula depending on how many races you've won. The apprenticeship period lasts a year from the date of your fifth win. Weight allowance seems to make a difference. You can be top apprentice in your salad days, but find few mounts sent your way in the journeyman stage.

Lucky owners float easily in and out of the racing world in their climate-controlled Cadillacs. They can decide to take the sport or leave it at any time. The typical backstretch boy doesn't have this option. Maybe racing has made him psychologically unsuited to everyday life. While the track is unlikely to pull anybody out of the trailer park and put him into a mansion, people just might find there the promise of belonging and of unending hope.

the great Nashua

WHIPPING BOY

Willie Davis was class. An exercise boy with a clock in his head that wouldn't quit.

"Take him to the 3/8 pole, set him down nice and easy in 36 and gallop out in 49."

Forget the stopwatch. He'd be right there.

Frank Whitely knew a good thing when he saw it. Workouts are tricky: go too slow and the horse gets nothing out of it; go too fast and the horse leaves his race—his piss and spunk—right there on the track.

Old Man Whitely was the devil to work for, but he and Willie went back a long time. What's more, he had the kind of high-class stock you'd die to lay your hands on.

One morning Willie came to work and ran into a killer. The horse was so rank he threw the boy 10 feet into a crumpled heap. Willie had been around long enough to know how to take care of himself, and he lay real still while the medics loaded him onto the stretcher and into the meat wagon.

"You lazy sonofabitch, lying down on the job! I got three more horses out here that need workin'."

With that Whitely collared Willie and dragged him from the ambulance. Willie got on two of them all right, but then the leg started to swell so bad they had to cut off the boot and hold that bone together with a horse bandage.

Women on the Track. Roughly ten years ago, jobs started cracking open for women because of the feminist movement which sought to instill a universal confidence that people can tackle whatever they set their minds to. Girls helped the backstretch: they cleaned it up, improved its image. Today you'll find exercise and pony girls, female hotwalkers, grooms, trainers, vets and jockeys. But lately there's been a subtle change. These women are a more seasoned and tougher type than the earlier teenaged horse enthusiasts. Marginal working conditions—hard work, low pay, poor accommodations—and the brutal side of racing have taken a toll on all but the gutsiest survivors.

Routines

A Day in the Life of a Racehorse. Horses apparently thrive on routine because that's what the backstretch is all about. Trainers would still have you believe that high technology and rare magic are involved in the conditioning of racehorses. It's an arguable point. What is true is that the endless variety of things that can go wrong makes this whole process much more sophisticated than auto mechanics. And, since two guesses are better than one, a good vet is as much a part of the shedrow as the horses themselves.

Stables differ in their make-up, just as mom and pop stores are distinct from giant corporations. Stalls are allotted before each meet through a byzantine process rife with cries of favoritism. If a trainer is known, liked and has a stable full of useful runners, there's rarely a problem. It's another story if you're newly licensed and applying for the first time at one of the more popular tracks. Your luck stands a better chance in the summertime when there are often several competing tracks open simultaneously, and all are combing the hills for horses.

A stable must move in its entirety from meet to meet unless it wants to settle for staying at a track which is currently not in session, but open for training year-round. This stable would then have to ship horses out to other tracks for races, which is inconvenient but manageable. Moving is obviously not a problem in localities which have just one track running for a full year's meet.

Large stables have an imperial trainer at the top who rules with the condition book. The foreman supervises the hands-on labor, the blood and guts of the operation. The grooms come next in line with two or three horses assigned to each as his direct responsibility. Hotwalkers are at the bottom of the pile, but usually rationalize their position as sort of an apprenticeship.

Except when a horse is singled out to race that afternoon or evening, the backstretch comes alive only in the morning. Night-racing tracks start their morning exercise sessions later, but the norm is a 5:30 a.m. first feeding. Horses will eat small meals throughout the day, depending on their digestive abilities.

It's time to tack up and get the first "set" of horses onto the track the moment the exercise boys come stumbling in. Not all horses are taken out for a gallop every morning. Fads change. The old method of two miles every day, rain or shine, has frequently been replaced by fairly light exercise scheduled for everyday horses who are already fit and racing regularly. A lot depends on soundness.

Shedrowing (walking around the shedrow with a rider up) or ponying (jogging a riderless horse alongside a lead pony) are a couple of easy alternatives. Galloping is still popular over shortened distances like one mile and a quarter, with a horse "blown-out"—worked for a quarter-mile or so—a few days before racing to build up high speed. The important point here is that any of these exercise regimes could fall by the wayside if the new Sportsmedicine approach gains acceptance. With its emphasis on fitness, exercise routines can be expected to get less rushed and more involved.

As it is, whenever the exercise boy drops his mount over to the rail, that's the signal to run: the horse knows he's not in for a saunter, but up for a "breeze" calculated to shake the trackside trees. Sometimes in the mornings, you'll see plastic traffic cones placed right along the rail to protect the hardest used part of the racing surface and confuse the situation. These cones are called "dogs." In the old days, mongrels used to patrol the infield making it advisable to keep away from the rail.

Any trainer would prefer to keep workout times out of print, particularly if he wants to slip a horse that's doing well into a cheap race. The timer is all-seeing from his perch in the grandstand and has an uncanny knack of knowing who's who. It always pays to scratch his back so that he will be sure to overlook a certain horse in the general confusion of the morning. The fastest work of the day, incidentally, is called a "bullet" workout and has a black dot printed beside it in the *FORM*.

The weather determines whether a hot and sweaty horse will be treated to a post-exercise bath. On cold days, a rubdown with a handful of straw does the clean-up trick if followed by a little extra currying. But there can be no getting around the holy tenet that all horses must be cooled out by walking the shedrow. Their bodies need a chance to clear cells gradually of the waste products of a heavy work. The walking ritual more or less prevents stiffness and soreness, and is a good time to check a horse out to see if the exercise brought to the surface any new problems.

The mechanical hotwalker is a cost- and labor-saving device that has come in for mixed reviews, mostly bad. It looks like a pared-down carnival ride: a pole trunk with limbs radiating overhead like the spokes of a wheel. A line is dropped from each limb to hook onto a horse, who is urged to plod around until cool. Horses don't like the monsters and can manage to mess up often enough so that most trainers would rather go broke paying human hotwalkers than stoop to using them.

Walking done, your horse will go back into the stall to nibble and pluck at his net of fresh hay, which is served along with the feed and water every morning. Although placing hay on the ground is more natural and promotes better drainage of the head passages, a hay-filled net hung outside the dutch doors encourages horses to look around and staves off boredom during the day.

Each horse gets special treatment around this time depending on his weakness or injury. Braces, liniments, sweats and poultices are dug out of the medicine chest, electronic gadgetry is hooked up and the 7–11 ice machine is raided for the cooling tubs. Fat stall bandages may be applied with a couturier's touch to keep in the heat or the cold and to protect against knocks. All this and more is known as "doing up." Spruced up and done up, a racehorse settles down to munch hay and daydream about fields of clover. During a hard campaign, he might even lie down and snore for about three hours.

A well-kept shedrow is a cosy scene. Horses seem to enjoy being surrounded by other horses and people. There is a feeling of being part of an important world, of doing things and going places.

Just about every horse appreciates a treat. The shedrow will focus on a carrot-laden visitor with the concentration of a tennis match crowd. Racehorses are generally lambs when off-duty, but you should find out beforehand which ones go in for being petted and which do not. There are always a few antisocial types and they could hurt you badly.

The predictability of the life which horses seem to thrive on points out as well as anything that horses are lovely animals, but not too bright. Sometimes a horse will have injuries so severe that he has to be confined to his stall around the clock for weeks on end. Most adjust well enough, and grow comfortable and secure in this set-up.

Few red-blooded horsemen believe in entertaining their horses by setting out towels to pull on or plastic bottles to bob. Yet horsemen will often turn in desperation to goats or cats as a calming influence, only to find that these relationships become a nuisance once the animals grow inseparable. Having to leave a friend serves to double racing's trauma. That's why it seems that hay all day long and into the night is the best comfort, short of TV, to head off the nervous types who like to weave (swing back and forth), crib (gulp air) or chew the wood off their stalls.

For years, horses have been expected to get and keep fit on the standard racetrack routine, even though it means about 23 hours a day in a 10 by 10 stall. In fact, there are iron horses who manage to race year-in, year-out without ever going sour or race-worn. Despite this, Sportsmedicine is stepping up to challenge tradition with the insulting intimation that the lead ponies may be fitter than the racehorses they babysit.

Race-Day

At the Barn. Routine around the shedrow on race-day varies surprisingly little from other days. A horse is usually given less exercise, hay, feed and water. Whether that horse will actually miss a meal depends on the time of the race. Trainers want to hold down intake for at least three to four hours before a race. Old-timers even used to cut way back on feed the day before, but drastic measures are weakening and unnecessary. Everything should be kept pretty much the same to avoid upsetting the horse, as long as he is not asked to run on a full belly.

If you are planning on shipping to another racetrack, the condition book will specify a time when all starters must be present on the grounds. This is generally two hours before post time. How much earlier you'll want to arrive depends on the horse. With a bad shipper who would fret in a new stall, arrive no sooner than the deadline. But for long hauls involving a particularly tough race and a seasoned veteran, you might do well to ship in a day early. The attendants—trainer, driver, groom, hotwalker (sometimes all rolled into one person)—will need extra pay for motel bills and meals and for hanging around the receiving barn. If it helps you win, go for it.

Certain horses need last-minute, pre-race attention. Sore legs can be packed in ice and then temporarily wrapped in cold bandages to keep the coolness in. Old campaigners might prefer to warm up their rusty limbs in the whirlpool— whatever works best in the morning gets repeated pre-race. Finally, ankles may need to be tightly wound with elastic racing bandages to provide support or prevent run-down injuries, which happen when skin is scraped off the bottom of a horse's ankle as he flexes to the ground. Racing bandages are pretty much of a necessary evil for sore horses. A sound horse will probably do better without them because they weigh down the legs, especially when wet.

Off to the Races. Racetrack help is punctual. There's no place for panic or nervous hands: time, tide and races don't wait. The backstretch PA system will announce exactly when horses must be brought over to the paddock for the next race. The trip proceeds with the pomp of a medieval processional.

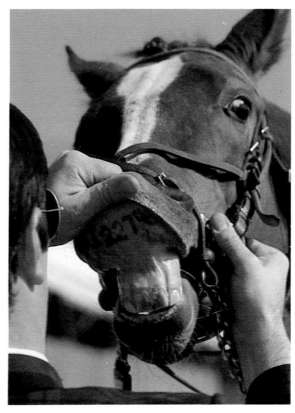

A nurse-maid pony will fall into step to escort the racehorse and his retinue right up to the paddock area. A pony can be any kind of cold-blooded horse that is trained to be calm, gentle and tough, sometimes with the help of a brutal bit. Each stable generally has its favorite pony and rider, and the pair is either part of the stable crew or freelance. These ponies are a purely American convention, practical and humane. No European track would allow the turf to be marred by anything other than the dainty hoof of a Thoroughbred racehorse.

Racehorses are as finicky as humans in their likes and dislikes. Love affairs are a common sight, with a racehorse chewing fondly on his favorite pony's mane. Annoyingly enough, there are other racehorses who will have nothing to do with ponies or a particular pony. The jockeys are the ones who suffer most without the support of a lead pony during the post parade and the warm-up period. Nothing is as exhausting as wrestling down a horse with racing on his mind.

151

Before the grooms are allowed to lead their horses into the paddock area, the horse identifier will flip over each horse's upper lip to doublecheck the registration number tatooed under it.

The jockey's valet should be ready and waiting in the paddock stall with the jockey's own saddle properly weighted and the saddle cloth bearing the post position number. Valets are no slouches: saddling a rampaging horse, not to mention keeping track of each jockey's costume and paraphenalia, calls for more than a little nimbleness.

Enter the Stars. Jockeys can be bantam roosters, but nobody belittles their role. Their moods, their whims are as crucial to winning as having the best horse entered: you can easily predict your luck when your jockey comes in muttering about how much money he just lost playing cards in the jock room. All jockeys have to be rounded up and isolated from an hour or two before their first race to the final race they're named in. But rather than helping the cause of honesty, this frequently long and boring confinement can be the perfect milieu for cooking up deals.

Especially on the smaller tracks, the pre-race scene has the look of a rodeo. The cowboy kings are the red-frocked outriders charged with keeping order, retrieving lost whips and so on. They periodically treat the crowd to a display of fancy horse-work by corralling a runaway horse or cajoling a reluctant runner through his paces.

Starting gate crews will remind you of speed-way pit-stop mechanics. They work with precision and know-how in an explosive arena. Horses go nuts easily, but never more so than during the loading of a well-filled race. Just one horse reluctant to go into the gate can set off all the others who are already loaded and impatient to be off. Men stationed inside the gate to hold the horses' heads have just enough time to run a quick mental check of their life insurance policies.

A man on each hind leg and a few more to shove is standard persuasion for a shy starter. Backing a horse into the starting gate also gets the job done as a last resort. Once in, a horse that rears in the gate or decides to sit down is a jockey-killer, and the common remedy for this is tailing. Holding up the tail is its mildest form. A crueler trick, twisting the tail, practically guarantees a walking start.

If your horse is a rogue, try to have him loaded last so that he'll have less time to mess up. Loading last often leads to starting first because a horse won't get settled in flat-footed. That's why, for a few extra bucks, pony boys can show great expertise at hiding their charges behind other horses. Don't worry, once any horse gets known as a knave, the starter will see to it that he goes in last or he doesn't get to go in at all.

The starter has to pick exactly the right second when all the horses are lined up noses straight ahead to press the button springing open the gates. The best jockeys at "sending" a horse will try to read the starter's mind and "break the gate" a split second ahead of electronics.

Holy Cows. Track stewards are awesome. Don't mess with them. A renowned and revered trainer once called them the "three blind mice" and earned himself a suspension. If you must question a call, brush up on the protocol for addressing royal personages. Better yet, take your lumps. The law of averages says that they'll bless you with a bad decision in your favor just as often as they stiff you.

EXILE

Gold Watch was a rough sort. Not too pretty. You might even call him a punk. But a record-breaking punk. High acceleration, flat-out speed. He'd been training continuously for over two years and was thriving.

The trainer's conscience came into play. Thought he ought to give the poor horse a break.

Gold Watch nibbled some grass and eyeballed the birds. He got bored and came back blah. Stuff your farm with country boys—this is one horse that wants to run.

155

Racing Care

A horse that's hitting his stride and winning with ease can be as unnerving as a no-win animal. You keep waiting for the other shoe to drop and for things to go wrong. Human instinct tries to prolong the winning streak by experimenting. This is the worst you can do. When you're winning with a horse, don't change a thing. Save your jolts for the horse that's slumping.

It is ten times better to keep a horse that's sound and happy in light training than to stop/start with him at arbitrary intervals. Bodies get flabby with disuse. Getting fit again can be slow and painful. Any athlete knows this.

Sportsmedicine. Racetrack life is thick with snake-oil salesmen and untested gadgetry. It's not so much a question of gullibility, but of pressure to find an edge. Horsemen are the first in line to try a new product and equally quick to discard it. Now there are rumors of a movement revolutionary enough to shake the foundations of Thoroughbred training. Like everything else, it should be considered even if horsemen choke on their belly laughs.

The idea of using the same scientific training methods which have successfully pushed human endeavor miles beyond all expectations is slowly infiltrating the racing world. This Sportsmedicine approach is not only innovative, it is complicated and expensive. Since most trainers are intuitive in approach and basically poor, inroads will be gradual.

One of the methods being given some play is the idea of basic conditioning through long, easy gallops. Horses have traditionally been worked that way in England, as have hunt racehorses in this country. It works best when training takes place off-track.

A radical view using this Sportsmedicine approach has horses galloping as early as the weanling year and eventually working up to some 10 miles a day, as opposed to the standard maximum of two miles for mature horses. Proponents breezily suggest that training fees should be doubled because the riders are expected to work longer and the animals eat more. But doubling the training bills for almost two years before a horse is ready to earn a dime would add up to an insupportable expense. The common practice of waiting until a horse is almost fully grown before subjecting him to tough training will probably remain strong, despite the claim that letting a horse work while he is growing will develop his body in concert with the motion.

Most horsemen agree that after boot camp a horse must be trained in the way he'll be racing. Sportsmedicine advises the use of interval training for revving up speed. Sprints are interspersed with rest periods for a distance of several miles. This graduated method keeps the horse from overdoing it and bringing on the injuries which go hand-in-hand with exhaustion. You've got to have a highly manageable horse, though, or it won't work.

The biggest drawback to Sportsmedicine is that American racetracks are not set up to accommodate a lengthy training process, in terms of hours per day and months overall. Tracks are only open for exercising horses from about six to 10 a.m. daily. On-track per diem is prohibitive, and Racing Secretaries are not crazy about barns full of training, but not racing, horses. The logical alternative is to do most of the conditioning on farms, but few trainers want to make the leap, especially the top ones who are treated like royalty on the track.

The development of Fair Hill in Maryland as an off-track training center in conjunction with the prestigious Fasig-Tipton auction house is a sign that change is not unthinkable. That—coupled with the impressive stakes runners pulled out of a hat by the country operation of Billy Boniface, another Maryland pioneer— has encouraged a proliferation of plans for more off-track centers in the U.S.

Aside from the greater flexibility in conditioning racehorses, the training center idea promises lower expenses, better barn help and less pressure from Racing Secretaries on when and where to run horses.

There are occasional signs that even track-based trainers are starting to go in for a modified Sportsmedicine approach. Dialectic theory dictates that every action brings on a reaction, out of which will emerge a workable compromise.

Hearts and minds are already turning in the right direction: proper training to prevent injuries beats the hell out of medicating them. Besides, with the hovering threat of federal legislation outlawing all medication, drugs may not always be a viable alternative.

Sportsmedicine has great potential for taking the guesswork out of horseflesh, from assessing potential to preventing, detecting and treating injuries. For example, someday soon you'll probably be able to predict where a horse's talents lie by analyzing the make-up of his muscle fiber. It has already taught some trainers to tell if a horse is getting fit by measuring heartbeat, which is as simple as taking a pulse. The possibilities are endless.

Experimenting with new theories is always risky: when things don't work out, trainers stand to catch the devil from hard-pressed owners. Even so, the Sports-

medicine approach cannot be ignored. It holds out hope for ultimately improving a stable's fortunes because it encourages horsemen to use the tools of science to understand and monitor racehorses in training. Life isn't simple anymore. There's not much room for the heavy-handed homilies that horsemen love.

Backstretch Basics

Nutrition. Racehorse diets have been fiddled with over the past ten years, but there haven't been many earth-shaking changes. Just as the recommended joggers' diet has gone from high protein to high carbohydrate, scientific research is trying hard to wean trainers away from feeding straight oats—which are a relatively hard-to-digest protein—in favor of high energy mixtures likely to contain molasses plus corn, beets, soybeans and the ubiquitous oats. Sophisticates may even dabble with glycogen loading schedules, but for most humans, nutrition is the great unknown. Witness how the latest vitamin, mineral and enzyme supplements are tried and discarded at a fast clip. Formulas tend to be clumsily balanced as well as expensive.

But one thing, quality hay, continues to be as much of a staple as fresh water for horses who need a little pampering with their pain. Racing has its compensations, and mealtime is one of the big ones.

Dentistry. Horse and dentist generally approach their first face-down over the biting issue of wolf teeth. These forward premolars can spell trouble when a horse starts working regularly in bridle and bit. They seem to serve no real purpose; they're in the way and are easily pulled out. Human health fanatics may claim that pulling teeth will weaken the brain, but in horses that's no great loss.

Around the age of three, a horse's permanent teeth come in, but it's not until age five that he has a full set. There can be 40 in all, counting 24 molars, 12 incisors, and four canines (in male horses and geldings).

These teeth keep growing. The softer parts wear down with years of grinding grain, leaving sharp enamel ridges. Trouble begins when these ridges stab at the tongue and cheeks. A strong-armed layman must be called in periodically to "float" the teeth, which means filing off the rough edges.

Shoeing. The awesomely fast but ill-fated racehorse, Cure the Blues, prods a thought about how many potentially good racehorses never had a chance because of weak feet. "No hoof, no horse" is right on the money.

Certain supplements will help harden hooves just as they can make people grow stronger nails. For more immediate results in toughening up soft hooves, you could even try applying layers of acrylic floor wax. Every trainer has a whole bag of these tricks and a crafty ally in his farrier, whose profession has grown increasingly sophisticated.

Farriers fall into philosophical camps. Some extremists believe in sculpting a short toe and high heel so that a horse will break over easier and faster, but land with a more jarring motion which tends to stress the joints. Others like a longer toe and lower heel which would lengthen the stride, but could put great pressure on the back tendons. There is also a lonely voice calling for the disuse of shoes entirely because shoeing would be something like putting cleats on a ballerina.

What *is* true is that shoes can be a drag. Exotic shoes custom-designed for problem feet often work beautifully to protect a weak spot, but manage to curtail running to a sedate plow-horse plop. Lightness should be the byword—"an ounce at the toe means a pound at the withers."

In a big stable, every horse gets a new pair of rubber-lined aluminum racing plates once a month, need them or not. There are some tracks which are so notoriously slippery that they call for mud caulks with stickers to get any kind of traction in the slop. But many smart trainers steer clear of these caulks for normal racing. They're one good way to come up with a broken hoof. Besides that, pulling shoes off to hammer on caulks the same day as the race is no longer done with equanimity. Every time you mess around with a hoof you weaken it.

Medication. To forestall the passage of a highly restrictive federal law, medication has been controlled in varying degrees, in various states, with variable success. A crusade was waged in the late '70s to outlaw all medication and return to racing on "oats, hay and water" alone. As noble a notion as you could ask for, it hanged itself in the web of its simplicity. Most horsemen feel that training horses ever so gently and running them so infrequently as to preclude any athletic soreness would financially break the racing industry. Horses have to run hard enough so that they can win often enough to pay their way. Just as in human competition, when you give it all you've got, sooner or later something's bound to give.

Horsemen, fighting for survival, have sought out other pain-relieving medications aside from the detectable controlled or outlawed substances. New medications far stronger, more physically detrimental and less fair to honest competition are being formulated just one jump ahead of detection technology. After reaping headache upon headache, horsemen and track management alike remember with longing the good old days of legal Phenylbutazone ("Bute") and Furosemide ("Lasix").

Bute has an anti-inflammatory and soothing effect on minor aches and pains, similar to aspirin, and is generally allowed to be used within certain limits during training, but no closer than 24 hours before a race.

Lasix usage rules are far more complex, and are spelled out in detail in each condition book. In many states, Lasix would only be permitted after a horse had been witnessed by the track vet to have bled from the nostrils after a race. A court order has now convinced more states to accept the results of scoping with high-tech instruments to determine if a horse has bled internally.

The controversy surrounding the use of Lasix is that it is not only a medication which seems to help bleeders, but also a diuretic which might mask a number of other drugs. It had once been assumed a horse's urine could become so diluted by all the water taken out of his system that no trace of illegal drugs would show up in a post-race test. There are indications now that new research may exonerate Lasix as a masking agent.

Trainers will often pass up the legally-sanctioned use of Lasix since it means sending a horse to the detention barn three to four hours before post time. Once there, some states prohibit any kind of pre-race preparation, even standing in ice.

Medication rules are in flux. The current program may not be a roaring success, but the threat of federal intervention could be enough to persuade states to tighten rather than abandon the regulations.

Racing Equipment. As an owner, you are not expected to become involved in buying most of the track equipment your horse will need. Your job is to foot the bills. Over the years, training outfits manage to accumulate a repertoire of equipment, both mundane and exotic, to fill every horse's needs.

Correcting Vices. Bridles are standard, but bits—the mouth pieces—are infinite in variety. Torture chambers have nothing on the stuff designed to discourage horses who have a tendency to lug in or drift out. It might be a psychological problem which makes a horse gravitate to where he feels most secure, but more than likely the horse is just trying to throw his weight off a sore side.

The eye pieces of blinkers can also be cut and sewn in crazy patterns to keep a swerving fool on the straight and narrow. But none of this equipment is foolproof. Nothing is worse than being saddled next to a horse in fancy headgear. You know you're heading for trouble—it's called getting blasted.

Finishing Touches. A horse might need special racing bandages to prevent run-downs or to support a weak point. He could also use a blanket to wear into the paddock during frosty weather. No need to worry about saddles: jockeys supply their own and the track puts out the numbered saddle clothes.

As a final piece of racing habiliment, a trainer will often pull a strip of cloth out of his back pocket to tie down a horse's tongue. It's a sticky and mutually unpleasant job, but necessary for sly horses who know how to work their tongues over the bit so that jockeys lose all control. Tying the tongue is also thought to help horses with wind problems by cutting down on obstructions. Nobody has told these guys yet that horses actually breathe through their noses, but it's still a good trick insofar as it keeps the throat's swallowing mechanism from blocking the windpipe.

Unique's the Thing. An owner can order—at his own expense—personalized equipment done up in his stable colors. Nylon bridles, blinkers, paddock blankets and exercise saddle cloths can easily be coordinated this way. Add a touch of class by ordering caps and jackets for the stable hands, complete with your racing logo. One enterprising owner went a step beyond by designing an equine jock strap to protect his oversized stallion, and matched it color for color with his racing silks.

○ Chapter Seven ○

CAN YOU MANAGE?

TRAINING YOUR TRAINER

Trainers are touchy. Most are closet Marlboro Men. Their profession encourages independence and a take–charge attitude because they are responsible from A to Z for thousands of dollars in horseflesh. No wonder it can go to their heads.

If your trainer treats you like a nuisance, it's time to find a new one. And it's surprising how many trainers still treat their owners like proverbial mushrooms, to be kept in the dark and fed horse manure.

Communication is all. You are depending on the trainer both to keep you apprised and to teach you. For your peace of mind, lay down the law on when you want to be called and how often. Otherwise you will find yourself hanging around the phone like a dateless teenager.

Any trainer who thinks he has a daytime job is deluding himself. The smart ones realize that a couple of hours spent on the phone each night touching base with some of their owners comes under the heading of a per diem expense. It's a service business.

Trainers will often avoid owners when things aren't going well. They don't know how to break the news. Let it be known that you want to be told the worst of it, that you want more than the usual platitudes ("The horse eats good and shits good"). If you show that you have a grasp of racing's problems, you'll break down a major barrier between owner and trainer.

Encourage your trainer to talk to you by making every conversation with him meaningful: quality conversation is geared to shed more light than a recitation of last night's bowling scores. Along this line, don't depend on him to tell you which horse made it into what race. You should already know beforehand where he intends to place each horse, and you can find out all about post positions and jockeys by calling the track yourself. Look to him instead for the important low-down on each horse, for his perceptions and for planning strategy.

Communication is followed by compromise. Trainers and owners are basically coming from different directions. You may want to give a horse that's slumping a nice, long rest, while the trainer is anxious not only to hang onto the incoming per diem, but to have enough warm bodies under his shedrow to qualify for x number of stalls in an upcoming meet. Or, he may have promised the Racing Secretary that your horse would help fill a race.

A good trainer wears two hats. He has to be a thoroughly competent and progressive horseman, and he has to be a clever and gutsy manager. A good horseman may be easier to come by than a smart manager brandishing a magical touch with the condition book. But don't even take horsemanship as a matter of faith.

Look into a prospective trainer's background and get some outside opinions on the quality of his work. Green owners are usually the ones who get stuck with bad trainers.

If a trainer vets out well as a conscientious horseman, you can easily help him out in the management department. As long as he is honest and you are realistic, you'll probably have the most fun with this arrangement.

Just as important as encouraging a good attitude in your horses is doing whatever you can to inspire your training outfit with confidence. Invite the trainer to your table. It's the perfect way to get a handle on each other: to gossip, celebrate a victory or discuss horsemanship and the condition book. You should train yourself to use initials or catch-phrases to identify the horses you are discussing. You never know who is sitting nearby in a packed trackside dining room, and the chances are awfully good that your competitors' hearing will be excellent and practiced.

It never hurts to be generous with your thanks and tips to the grooms and support troops. It always pays off well in that sunny bit of extra attention for your horses.

THE BOSS

Interview With Fred W. Hooper
Breeder and Owner Par Excellence

TR: I take it you have a lot of input with your trainers.

Hooper: That's one of the reasons I've had so many young trainers with me, because I can talk to them. I'm not abusive or anything like that. But as long as I pay the bills I'm going to have something to say about it. Many owners turn a lot of money and a lot of horses over to trainers and let them run the whole thing. The same people wouldn't turn their businesses over to their employees.

TR: You've had a number of trainers over the years. Are you a hard man to train for?

Hooper: No, I don't think so. But regardless of the trainer I'm going to be able to talk to him or he won't train for me. Some trainers don't want their owners around the barn.

—Courtesy of THE THOROUGHBRED RECORD

©DAILY RACING FORM

PAPERWORK

Resist the temptation to nap. There's no way around paperwork. While it's relatively easy to keep tabs on a one-horse stable, when you've got twenty, you'll need accessible figures to know where you stand.

Racing has to be accountable as a business. This is the only way to keep from ricocheting back and forth between fantasy and reality. It has outgrown the image of a gentlemanly dalliance.

Crying Time

At the end of each meet, the track bills you for any expenses not covered by the winnings shifting through your account. The Horsemen's Bookkeeper tallies in jock fees and charges for as many win pictures as you've chosen to order. (See Appendix.) Nice-guy owners generally find themselves buying pictures for the trainer, the jockey and a handful of strangers who've slipped into the ring.

Lead pony fees are often standard items. This fee was originally imposed to discourage the use of lead ponies because they make it harder for the bettors to check out the horses. Now that almost everybody uses a pony, the Horsemen's Benevolent & Protective Association in some states can depend on these fees as a source of steady income.

Trainers bill monthly. If you make the trainer your authorized agent, he can draw money from the winnings in your account to cover his bill or claim in your name. Play it safe and wait until you know him well before indulging in this convenience.

The trainer's bill typically includes board, his percentage of the winnings (10%), farrier charges, vanning expenses and another lead fee which is actually paid to the pony boy. Vet bills are too huge for him to carry.

Systems

Memory Bank. It's a good idea to start off by buying a pack of three by five index cards. When a horse runs, copy down the pertinent information before your wastebasket gets emptied, then file away the cards chronologically. Likewise, prepare cards for whenever a horse is bought or sold, he's born or he dies, and store these in another file. This is your memory bank. (See Appendix.)

Computer Fun. To keep the financial picture highly—if painfully—visible, a comprehensive debit and credit sheet covering each and every horse should be prepared monthly. Use your memory bank to supply you with the amounts won by the individual horses and their race-day expenses. Tally in recent acquisition costs or selling gains. Next, grab each bill as it comes in and break out each horse's board and training costs, farrier fees, medical expenses and so on. With a little first-grade computation, you should be able to come up with a monthly plus or minus earnings figure for every horse in every division (breeding, racing or lay-up) and for your overall racing operation. These figures can easily be crunched through a computer to prepare more brutally revealing analyses like the year-to-date profit or loss picture on a particular animal. That's when the comforting haze parts and you'll know just how deep in the dung you're standing. (See Appendix.)

Money, money, money . . .

IN THE PICTURE

Question: "What's the most expensive thing about racing?"

Answer: "The win picture. Each one costs thousands without the frame."

Then you can comfort yourself by looking at your company line:

Annual negative cash flows of $20,380,200 for NYRA and Finger Lakes horsemen in 1980 have been calculated by comparing total purses with total training costs. These negative cash flows occur before any allowances for depreciation or purchase of horses. Furthermore, while substantial revenues are generated from the sale of horses for breeding, the New York horsemen still incurred an additional negative cash flow of approximately $20,000,000 for the purchase of horses in 1980.

—Courtesy of the New York Division, Horsemen's Benevolent & Protective Association

Tax Work. You can use the cash method of accounting for small farm operations, family corporations or Sub-chapter S corporations (where losses or profits spill over to personal taxes, but liability is limited to the company). Be sure to buy a fancy ledger to log in all the expenses incurred by your racing venture for the amusement of your taxman. This log book can be set up by your accountant so that expenses are broken down into standard categories like insurance, operating supplies, vanning and the like. Also keep on hand an appointments' calendar to keep track of your travel mileage for racing-related errands. The government allows a fixed deduction per mile, and you'd be surprised how fast it adds up.

When you buy racehorses—not for resale but to "place into service"—you can depreciate them in five years' time, or in three years for horses over two years old. Capital gains treatment applies for racehorses owned for 24 months, which means that you can deduct 60% of the gain. The saddest part of equine tax law is that a nice 10% investment tax credit can't be taken on horses like it can on other livestock.

Incidentally, the loss you deduct per year can never exceed the total amount you had "at risk." But losses can be suspended and allowed for the following year if you're still in the business.

The key to remember about taxes is that if you're in racing for the tax shelter alone, real estate would suit you better. But if racing happens to be the most challenging world you've ever accosted, you deserve a break. The hobby loss provision—is it a business or is it a hobby?—will be your biggest hurdle.

There are nine ways of determining if your operation is for real, if you expect it to profit and grow. Quickly, they are:

1. businesslike records and efforts to improve profitability,
2. your know-how and that of your advisors,
3. attention given the enterprise,
4. your hope that the assets will appreciate in value,
5. your overall success in life,
6. profit/loss history of the horse operation,
7. relative size of profits to losses,
8. outside income and tax shelter motive, and
9. how much fun you're having.

Be sure to appear unhappy and frazzled when the auditor comes around. Look suitably earnest—particularly if you haven't cleared a good profit two out of seven years.

Insurance. Insurance is a hot topic, a must-have among the upper reaches of Thoroughbred stock. Most claiming level horses frankly aren't worth it. They may be here today and gone tomorrow. They're always being moved up and down in the ranks to find the best spots, which makes it hard to pinpoint their value. What's more, the procedures involved if an animal has to be destroyed can be a mess. No matter how good the terms, insurance companies give nothing away.

'WELL, AT LEAST WE CAN SAVE HIM FOR STUD...'

Files. Aside from keeping your financial structure clear and easily accessible, you'll need to stay on top of the paperwork involved in registering and naming foals, entering stud animals into the record, renewing licenses and the like. As long as you have made up individual folders with the lowdown on every horse, these procedures are fairly simple.

Systems vary, and yours will evolve. But a figure scribbled here or there on the back of an envelope won't do the job. Start out with accurate record-keeping before the fast action of an active claiming stable whirls you away into a hopeless muddle. Horses multiply like rabbits.

UNDERSTANDING THE GAME

"How to ruin a good horse" is a subject you're sure to become an expert on during your racing career. Horses are ruined through human error, ignorance and insensitivity about as often as commuters miss their buses. Horsemanship is only part of the problem; faulty guesswork is the other. You have to understand that nature believes in compensation, that a horse who might not be much in one capacity may be great in another. The idea is to pinpoint your horse's best shot. Pedigree, conformation and performance will give you clues. Be observant. Once you've found that winning mode, don't ask your horse to do anything else.

The better a horse is in talent or class, the less susceptible he is to the varying conditions of each race. But the unhappy fact is that so much and so little can cause most horses to conclude that racing is no fun. Being wrongly spotted, badly bumped or poorly ridden can irrevocably ruin most Thoroughbreds. The breed is fundamentally timid.

Recognizing your horse's racing niche is one way to promote a productive racing career. Catering to non-racing considerations is another. Does he like his groom? Is his hay placed where he wants it? Horses can be as picky and as fretful as humans. That's why nothing delights a trainer more than a good "doer," a mesomorphic creature who loves his grub and doesn't think too much.

LIKE GANGBUSTERS

Abu Dhabi. Moved like a dream, ate like a pig, could have been great. Like a lot of talented horses, he didn't like to mess around with people. Lived in his own world. Not mean, just aloof.

Bought cheap as a weanling for $1300, as Abi grew so did our expectations. You could see by his effortless motion and self-contained style that he was going to be nice. Some things are obvious. You'll know it right from the start.

The horse suffered from terminal mismanagement. It took too many wasted races to figure out his style. He loved a hard, fast track, getting an easy lead over distance of ground and being held under a steady rein. Not unusual—if you think about it. In time he got discouraged, got known as a quitter from being badly spotted.

There came a turning point in Abu Dhabi's life when he was finally starting to mature and to toughen. Worst luck, his race turned up on a deep and sodden Bowie track . . . but right down the middle was an asphalt-hard path.

It won't change history, yet we'll never forget it. Abi, the gutless wonder who hated the hurly-burly of being back in the pack, hated the mud in his face, was actually coming on like a freight train right down that path. He was closing, and closing fast, when the bug-boy jockey forgot his instructions and dropped over to the security of the rail. The rail was deep, the mess horrible and Abi's courage forever blown.

Horses can be taught and boats can be caught, but not this time.

Condition Books

The next few pages are custom-tailored to confuse the casual race-goer. They wade into the weathered channels of a racetrack mind. Horsemen know that spotting your horse in the right race is about 60% of a win and it gives them plenty to ponder during the long idle hours. Learning to practice some cagey precepts will put you on the path to becoming a racetrack mogul.

Tracks periodically issue booklets which set out the conditions of the probable races scheduled for each race-day over the next two weeks or so. The Racing Secretary's biggest job is to compile this condition book so that it meets the needs of the racehorse community. (See Appendix.) For example, two-year-old races are rarely in demand in the Mid-Atlantic states until April or May, and it isn't until the bulk of the two-year-old crop starts coming to hand around September, that you find two-year-old races carded with any great regularity.

You used to be able to order condition books simply by calling the Office of the Racing Secretary at any racetrack. Some tracks would even put your name on a mailing list so that condition books could be automatically sent to you as soon as they came out. These courtesies have by and large gone the way of the dodo bird in the interests of economy.

The HBPA Office is now your best bet. They stock condition books for all the area tracks. If they don't happen to carry books for a distant track, then it's up to you to wheedle one from that track. You might have to pretend you are a trainer to qualify for receiving a book. This reflects the prevailing attitude that owners should be kept well out of it for everybody's peace of mind.

While you are busy studying the condition books from all the tracks within shipping distance looking for the perfect race, glance over their rules to see if there are any unusual regulations on medication, scratchtime or claiming policy. Nobody needs this kind of surprise.

Staying on top of the condition books is the strength of any winning stable. Unfortunately, trainers vary greatly in their expertise with the clumsy catchphrases. While it's not unusual to find a trainer who considers the condition book his private domain, an owner's two cents' worth can be counted on to give any trainer greater perspective. That's why it's important to make a point of discussing racing options with your trainer on a week-by-week basis, weighing the pros and cons. Several races can seem equally attractive in different ways, even if neither of you can find the perfect one.

Races can be differentiated not only by claiming price, but by age, sex, length, and number or amounts of wins within a specified period ("the conditions"). Entries are usually taken a couple of days before each race is to be run. The race of your choice may not fill—track officials usually want at least six or seven starters—or may overfill. In that case, your horse may get a "star" for preferential treatment next time around. Post positions are drawn at this time, but can be lowered because of scratches.

Conditions can be as important as claiming levels. Horses who haven't won often should look for races restricted on the basis of wins, so that they won't have to go against any tough old winning campaigners. Some talented veterans may be running on deflated claiming levels because age and its attendant frailties will suffice to frighten off buyers at any price. Let observation and experience guide you to the protected plums.

Condition books have a rhythm of their own, meaning that the same races will generally reappear at two-week intervals. If your stable is turning over gradually with the successful animals progressing from, say, "non-winners of two races" to "non-winners of three races," you won't need to run back in the very same race every other week. Otherwise, you should do a little creative thinking to find a more advantageous spot if the race at a certain level keeps on coming up unusually tough with the same bunch of horses. Skip a week and lock-step with a weaker field.

The key to good management is learning to spot your horses well. One trend-setter used to scandalize old-time trainers by spending each morning—primetime on the backstretch—snug abed with the condition books. His capable assistant kept him abreast of any new developments in his stable. This arrangement was highly effective: King Leatherbury became the nation's leading trainer and revamped the image of a trainer into one smart businessman.

Shipping. There is a favorite wives' tale that once you put a horse on a trailer, it makes no difference how far you ship him. Don't believe it for a minute. The starting, turning and stopping force even four-legged creatures to shift back and forth for balance and comfort. It is nerve-racking and tiring, though it beats hoofing it.

If you are going after a particularly big purse, take all the precautions to make the trip worthwhile even if it means shipping up a day early. This way you can tranquilize a problem shipper during the trip. But know your horse. If he looks like a stall worrier, there's no point in stirring him up any earlier than usual.

There's one thing you don't want to do, and that is to bring your own jockey up with you. Unless your horse is the devil to ride, use the local talent. They know the track inside and out. If you've been shipping in nice horses to win with, not just culls to lose through the claim box, they'll remember and respect you. And in the event that your horse comes up empty, you won't have to feel guilty about forcing your own jock to climb mountains to be there. Nor will you find a bill in your mailbox for dinner for two at the Oak Room and ticket stubs for Plato's Retreat. Plus airfare, privately chartered.

Comparative Shopping. You have to weigh the relative strength of competition at each track to know where to place the horse you intend to ship. For example, a race with a medium-range price tag would usually not draw the same level of competition at Laurel, Keystone or the Meadowlands. The Laurel horses might have the edge over the Meadowlands horses who would in turn be likely to edge out the Keystone horses.

Maryland racing is especially tough at Laurel and Pimlico despite the fact that purses can run larger at both the Meadowlands and Keystone. High standards are set by the top trainers who make their homes wall-to-wall in the Free State. They are lured there, in part, by an accommodating management which helps them out with plenty of stall space. Although not exactly movie star types, they stand to make a good living by matching wits with each other, guile by guile.

Expensive and cheap are also defined differently at each track. At the moment, running on claiming levels above $10,000 pretty well protects a nice horse at a country track, just as anything over $20,000 is probably safe at a mile track in Maryland. This in turn would be considered a low and active claiming level at tracks nearer to New York, where horsemen are used to spending and earning top dollar.

In the shadowy world of horse racing, trainers come full of superstition and foreboding. If you are bent on getting the best performance out of each horse in your shedrow, the trainer must be weaned of his prejudices against shipping to this or that track. The only foibles that should be honored are the horse's. "Horses love courses" refers not so much to the lucky aura surrounding a track, as to the way each track suits a horse's running style.

ANGEL

CHRIS

BOTTOMING OUT

Summertime is shipping time. Holiday tracks bang open their gates to offer horsemen a smorgasbord of purses and conditions to choose from. Horse vans and RV's clog the highways.

We'd been in the game a good while then, long enough to realize that any extra fuss and preparation an owner goes through before a race can serve to deepen the disappointment afterward. Going racing should be a spontaneous thing, as natural and simple as walking out the door.

Still, the spot was a sweet one and our horse was dependably full of a winner's fire, so we thought nothing of catching a couple of planes just to see him run. Besides, by then we figured we'd seen it all. Had posted enough lightning rods to guide racing's shocks harmlessly to ground.

Couldn't help it. The excitement was infectious. A beautiful day was topped by the feeling of being free, playing hooky from the serious business of living.

Soon after the old prop hunkered down for a Rickettyback landing, a messenger elbowed his way up the gangplank waving a hastily scrawled note:

"Van mishap. Horse reared, struck head. He's dead."

We reboarded the plane for the long flight home.

177

How to Choose A Race

The tracks need a steady supply of horses to fill races and horsemen to foot the bills. The best suggestion in years is that the tracks should pay an owner every-time he starts a horse. Owners supply the gladiators for the big fight and, without them, there could be no racing. Tracks see things the other way around, so winning races (or selling horses) is still the best way to make money.

Claiming Levels. Spotting races for claiming level horses will be your initial passion. Once you have mastered that, choosing the right allowance and stakes race for your better stock will seem like a cinch since finding the best conditions and the worst competition will then be your only concerns. In the beginning, though, claimers will constitute the mainstay of your stable. Don't wince. Understandably, nobody ever wants to think that their stable will be ordinary in any way. Sometimes yes, sometimes no . . . there are plenty of talented horses running in claiming ranks. The most illustrious graduate of all is John Henry, Horse of the Year in 1981 and winner of over $4 million. He once ran for a tag of $20,000. Some horses just need a change of connections, a fresh approach or a little better care in order to improve.

It bears repeating: good management means placing your horses in races they can win. Consider the level, consider conditions. To do this, you must have a realistic assessment of a horse's value, which you can only make if you excise your ego from your racing decisions. Will Rogers notwithstanding, it is possible for a good man to come up occasionally with a bad horse.

'HE RALLIES NICELY...'

Unproductive racehorses are expensive hot potatoes to get stuck with. They can cost as much as the good ones to maintain, and possibly more in terms of attention, medication and anguish. This realization should give you the freedom to play the claiming game with abandon and a resolve to win.

Horses are investments. The most common pitfall comes when an owner gets too high on a horse and moves that horse stubbornly up to his level of incompetence. Unlike children, racehorses should be encouraged to run in the worst possible company. Stick them in with the dolts and oafs where the winning is easy. Don't pit them against the class president.

Only if you have championship material may you be forgiven for wanting to indulge in the sportsman-like thrill of accepting any challenge in the land. Even so, there are few owners of any top class racehorse today who would be willing to risk sure defeat. Resale value and stud fees could nose-dive. It would tarnish a sterling image.

You'll find that it is never humiliating or uninteresting to run and win, even at the cheapest level. If you're involved with your animals, each race will be as compelling as the Kentucky Derby. Winning is a miraculous accomplishment! Aside from talent, an unruly mix of variables—a favorable track, a good trip and so on—all have to coalesce for that win picture. That's why only about 10% of the hopefuls going to the post come back as winners.

How Sore, How Old. When deciding which level to go in, consider how vulnerable your horse is in terms of soundness and age. There is no point in running your horse against heavy competition if he's sure of a win and relatively safe from being claimed on a lower level. The many races you could conceivably win with him on an easy level might offset the bigger purses he might occasionally be able to win on a higher level. Easier races will probably take less out of him so that you'll be able to prolong his racing career.

At the bigger tracks, horses are generally considered old earlier, since few can take the stress of top-level racing for long. Although some horses can successfully extend their usefulness with a less rigorous campaign at a smaller track, no horse can last forever. A veteran over nine is virtually untouchable anywhere, although a horse can live to a ripe old age of 30, which would be something like 90 human years. Few people can afford to "eat a horse," a crudely put way of saying that they must write off his cost when he can no longer race.

Despite all this, it's easy to develop a soft spot for racing veterans. No exasperating schooling races are necessary. All you have to do is keep them reasonably fit and comfortable: when the starting gate opens, they know exactly what to do. Some have been running in claiming races that have actually come up tougher than allowance fields, which now and then are filled with namby-pamby well-breds being protected for their residual value in the breeding shed.

Not even young horses can be expected to run every two weeks ad infinitum. They all need freshening from the physical strain of racing. A horse might run the equivalent of six months each year during his career. During the time that he's "on," he has to win enough to cover his purchase price and then the full year's board, plus vet and incidental expenses, to break even at year-end. Knowing that you need people to claim away iffy horses that might not otherwise be able to balance their accounts will assuage the pain of having someone claim a nice horse off you. You can never afford to look back in anger.

'CLAIMED AT LAST'

How Expensive. If you paid an inordinate amount for a horse, you'll be tempted to recoup your lunatic investment by protecting him from being claimed from you at too cheap a level. But trying to nickel and dime back as much as you can through winnings could actually be false economy. Experience shows that an unpromising horse should be sold while he's still a saleable commodity—wait too long and everyone else will realize he's a bum. The few purses he may eke out for you at a higher claiming level will probably be far less than what you could realize if you dropped him to a lower claiming level, where you might have a good shot at picking up both the claiming sale price (if somebody falls for him) and the win purse. Not to mention saving the subsequent board and vet bills. If you do not try to sell a run-of-the-mill racehorse at some point through the claim box, not only will you pass up here-and-now money but you may even get stuck paying for that horse's vacation or retirement plans.

Running a horse in expensive company rarely improves the quality of his talent; in fact, it may discourage any initiative he has. Racehorses are performance animals and each one deserves a shot at success, however humble the level.

How Talented. How Hopeful. The axiom "run your horses as cheaply as you can" should apply to at least 90% of your claimers. There are always going to be some horses that you suspect have enough talent worth protecting until they "come to hand" by growing more race-wise or greyhound fit. This applies mostly to young horses and brand-new stock.

There are also horses which you will admittedly single out to protect because of emotional attachment. When you've been around the track a few times, though, these pets will dwindle with the realization that the only horses worthy of your time, care and money are those that will win for you. The underlying idea is to win and make enough money to stay in the business so that you'll be there when the big horse comes along.

Conditions. Ferreting out the sweet racing spots for your horse takes judgment and imagination. Take advantage of a conditioned race: if the glass slipper fits, wear it.

The smaller tracks regularly card not only conditioned claiming races for maidens (non-winners), but also those restricted to non-winners of two or three races. Restrictions may be either lifetime or refer to the amount of races won within a certain period. As mentioned earlier, the level of competition in this kind of restricted race can be immeasurably weaker than running in wide-open company. Horses that haven't won much are easy pickings compared to the hard-knocking winners who just happen to be running cheap because of age or infirmity. By the same token, races restricted to state-breds or to female horses can usually be counted on to come up softer.

No wonder handicappers snicker at befuddled owners. When a horse "breaks his maiden" (wins his first race), chances are that his connections will run him back at a much higher level. Unless this first win was convincing enough for Derby aspirations, just graduating into open company would be a step up in class and enough of a challenge for any horse.

The Luck of The Draw

Post position can decide a race even before it begins. A crushing inside post when the race starts on a straightaway, or a wide-swinging, outside post when starting on a turn can be the kiss of death. Only horses who are overwhelmingly the best or have enough early speed to maneuver quickly into good position can count on overcoming rotten post positions. (See Appendix.)

A trick that might ensure an attractive post position is to submit an entry of two horses for a race and scratch the horse with the worst position. You'll never have trouble scratching part of an entry. This is because the horses in an entry always carry the same odds, so that your scratch wouldn't affect the total betting choices. For this reason, no entries are ever accepted in exotic betting races like trifectas and daily doubles. Entries would cut down on the betting play.

Short fields can be a real blessing from the horse's standpoint. Think of how much easier it would be to maneuver into position in a field of six runners as opposed to 12. The chances of a clean trip are infinitely greater, particularly for closing horses who face a wall of backsides to wiggle in, out, around and through.

Despite the advent of year-round racing, there's still a seasonal flux in the quantity of horses stabled on the track. Mid-winter fields can be light because harsh weather is rarely conducive to good racing. The best horses are frequently mothballed, while colds and injuries from frozen tracks and flying debris take a toll on the lesser ranks.

Summertime racing can be equally uncomfortable, although night racing helps even the score. Horses, like humans, tend to get sluggish in the heat, especially those suffering from breathing difficulties. But, because more tracks stay open during the summer season to compete for the holiday dollar, the resultingly thin fields and ready purses make it hard to resist running horses throughout the summer, despite oppressive weather. Of course, if your stock is worthy of Saratoga, it's never a hardship to run horses there.

Autumn and spring are a different story. Not only do the big boys come out to play, but every little rat is given a now-or-never shot. The star wars begin. If your horse is excluded from an overfilled race, he might automatically be given a star for special consideration next time around. He'll then be placed on the "preferred" list. This star will help him get into any claiming race within a $500 spread from the previously entered level. Sometimes that's not enough: first consideration will be given to horses with two or three stars.

Competition for entry gets particularly heady at the small tracks toward the end of autumn when starving outfits are desperate to reel in some money before winter's setbacks set in. One memorable race on the bottom once filled with 10 in, four on the also-eligible list (these horses have a shot of getting in if there's an early scratch) and 82 horses excluded.

RACING

The Inputs

People outside of racing naturally assume that the fastest horse in any given race wins. But since racehorses can be evenly matched in talent, other factors come into play. Factors like circumstantial luck and the strength of the human connections. Not to forget each starter's fitness and soundness, his freshness and state of mind.

Wave-lengths. Horses have their own ways of going into a race. If you know your horse pretty well, you can tell when he's ready to run. The ideal paddock behavior comes from a horse who's alert, head up and looking around. Slight tremors of excitement and lashing out with the hind legs are fine signs. "Kidney sweat" foam might even show up between the rear thighs as tension mounts. It's never comforting, but sometimes normal, for a horse to be "washed out" with rivulets of sweat running down his neck and belly. It's much worse to see a horse so quiet he's headhung.

Blows can come from infinite sources to challenge an owner's dream of a winning streak. At some tracks, the bias can change from day to day as management over-corrects a too fast or too slow track. The only way to keep sane is to have a little diversity built into your stable so that at least some of your runners will have a shot at winning on any particular day.

Owner anxiety builds as the time grows short before each race. You'll have to teach yourself the fundamentals of equanimity: after scratchtime, accept weather and track conditions with fatalism. Worry about the few factors you can still control.

The trainer has the podium in giving the jockey race instructions. Discuss these with him beforehand or you might find yourself standing by helplessly as he explains some off-the-wall plan. Listen carefully. The trainer is not infallible—he might forget something or get his horses mixed up.

Sometimes throwing the jock a well-considered comment— "Did you know that this horse once held a track record?"—will do wonders. If you exude a worthy confidence, the grooms and the trainer will pick up on it and so will the featured players, your horse and his jock.

Owners reach a point where nothing gives them the jitters so much as a race that is shaping up perfectly. A horse doesn't always acknowledge his good luck, and now he's got fewer excuses to fall back on. Once your racehorse is out on the track, there's nothing more you can do: it's his show.

It's worthwhile to invest in the best pair of binoculars that you can lay your hands on. During the race is no time to play a guessing game about where your horse is running. You can't always rely on the announcer or the TV monitor because they will focus mainly on the horses out in front.

185

Trip. You'll know you're a horseman when you can walk in off the street and follow any race, without knowing a single thing about the runners. You'll be able to appreciate the unfurling drama, especially when two horses run head to head, vying for the lead. A willful battle between evenly matched horses can sometimes carry the dueling pair far beyond their natural abilities. Symbiotic momentum spurs them on.

Veteran race-watchers can usually pinpoint the instant a contest is won or lost. There is a caving in, a micro-second of submission, which can seem as arbitrary as the flip of a coin. That's why the true sign of a class horse is that he will look a competitor in the eye and not back down. The same rituals of confrontation and submission are practiced every day in a free-running herd.

Some of the most frustrating horses in your barn will be those who won't run a lick if they don't get the lead. This is a common quirk, particularly among young horses who run scared. Their races will be decided by the break and the first few strides. If a clear lead is gained, their hearts will grow big and you can relax as long as the track bias is not dead set against them. The best ones will fight hard to hang on.

This all-or-nothing mentality turns up time and again. Over the years, horsemen have learned to accommodate it. It automatically lowers the class of a horse a notch or two since he must run against weaker competition to ensure that he can nab an easy lead. If your horse doesn't have the kind of early speed needed to grab the lead in a sprint, you could try training him to run in longer races. The pace of a distance race is slower in the early fractions, so that it could be easier to assume the lead while most of the field is saving its strength for the miles ahead.

Pace can be cunningly played with during classically longer races. Top-notch jocks are experts at slowing down the fractions once they have wrestled the lead, just so the frontrunners can loaf along and still be fresh at the end. Nobody would be willing to waste energy contesting the lead too often in a race that goes on for a mile or more.

Although frontrunners win their share of races, you'll welcome a horse with a more flexible running style, such as one that would allow him to stalk the leaders by laying a close third or fourth in the clear—not contesting the pace, but never letting the leaders get too far in front. This way, the horse could stay relaxed all the way around and save his energy for a kick at the end. It is a modus operandi that would make a horse more independent of the track bias than speed horses who must rely on a hard track or field-trailing closers who look for a heavy-going surface to bog down the frontrunners. But, your horse is still not home free: he's liable to run into traffic problems, especially on the rail. Yet if he runs on the outside, it would mean that he won't have been able to save much ground. Getting a good trip is rarely a cinch.

Running styles are seldom taught. Good handling and training may give a horse the confidence to relax during a race, while sensitive hands on a jockey can orchestrate racing tactics to his greatest advantage. Basically, though, running style is ingrained in a horse's physical type, talent and personality. Does he show natural speed or must he rely on endurance to mow the others down? How competitive and aggressive is he? Can he be counted on to hold his own?

No matter how versatile and manageable a horse may be, any winning effort is helped by a boy up who knows and likes the horse. It's tough to win a race with a last-minute jockey change, even if the horse is odds-on favorite. Newly-appointed jockeys are mentally unprepared.

Results. Any time a horse comes in on the board (one through four), it's a good road sign that he's been placed right, that the race was suited to his talent and condition. If he does poorly, consider the possibility that he is ill or injured, as well as badly spotted. Calculate how far he was beaten. Was it by a nose, head, neck, half-length or several lengths? You can find out how fast your horse ran by figuring that he would have been 1/5 second slower than the winning time for each length he was beaten in a six furlong sprint.

Second place is the consolation prize. The compensation for coming in an uninspiring second is that you can cut down appreciably on your expenses. You'll get a smaller percentage of the purse than the winner, but at the big tracks this is still real money, considering that you don't have to pay out large chunks to the jockey, trainer, barn help and photographer. It's cold comfort any way you slice it: you can't hang seconds on your wall.

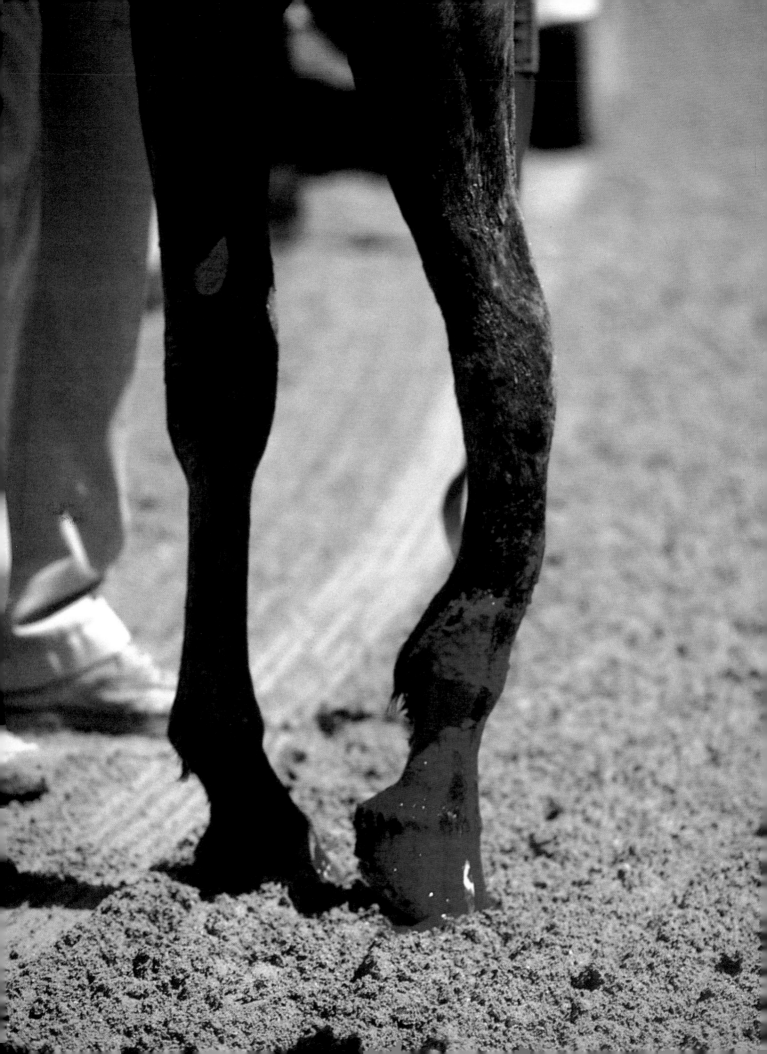

THE BREAKS

Racing, as everyone knows, is comprised of victory and defeat. They come at once: for every winner, there are many losers behind him. Disappointment one day heightens the pleasure of success on another day; except when there can be no other days . . . .

When anticipation ends, when ability and class are not enough, when strength ebbs, when bone shatters, when rhythmic beauty sprawls, and the heart is stopped.

Talent is important, but luck is essential in racing, and Timely Writer was a star-crossed colt . . . .

They all ran over the same cuppy track. Only Timely Writer took a bad step. We know not how to explain it, other than he had bad luck. He had courage, he had speed, he had class. He was good, maybe the best, but he was unlucky. And he raced against that, every step of the way, to his last.

Kent Hollingsworth

—Courtesy of THE BLOOD-HORSE

Damage

Early Warning. A horse is usually too "up" for any minor race–related injuries to become noticeable immediately after a race. You'll know, though, the minute he pulls up if he's not fit—he'll have a crease down his back and be blowing hard. Some horses stay exhausted for days. They will not "clean up," they shun their food in favor of curling up and resting. A race can take so much out of a horse that most trainers go easy for a while by walking a horse around the shedrow instead of training.

Stay on the lookout for trouble if your horse ran a rough race. At high speed, any abrupt maneuvering, shoving or pulling up will distribute a horse's weight unevenly and could put pressure on a susceptible area.

You'll definitely know something's wrong if your horse seemed reluctant to change leads during the race. A horse gallops with one of its front legs ahead of the other, "leading" as it scrapes up the ground. Most horses reach for a burst of speed by changing to a fresh lead as they round into the homestretch. If a horse doesn't change leads freely back and forth during a race, he's favoring a sore spot.

Analyzing physical problems with a scientific frame of mind, you'll see that horses lean hardest on their healthy wheels. The rundown bandage which has been worn through on one side shows up a problem on the other side. Horses that habitually lug in or duck out during races may merely be shifting weight off a sore side.

Whenever a horse is seen "pointing" in his stall, standing with one foreleg ahead of the other while resting, there's trouble afoot. Sound front legs lock upright to rest easily. The hind legs are a different mechanism—healthy horses habitually shift weight from side to side to relax.

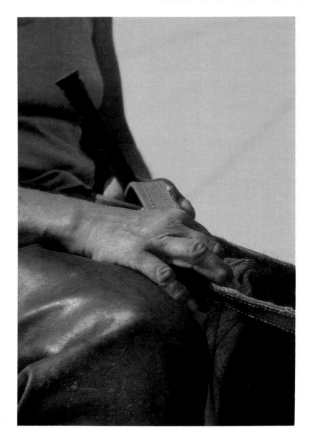

In a better world, horse and human could moan to each other about troubles and pain. As it is, most people don't take the time they should to explore and assess the extent of injuries, both obvious and exotic. Be sensitive. Too many horsemen blithely assume that any reticent animal just has a poor attitude and needs a little more racing to fire his enthusiasm. Does the horse really lack heart or is he actually sore? It's worth finding out.

The drop in class that horses undergo once they start having problems is breathtaking. With fewer than four legs, a horse can't run well regardless of ability. A horse might win easily against $20,000 horses, but once the hurting starts, barely make it against $2,000 claimers.

Troubles. Every groom can point out a full-range of exotic ailments being treated at the shedrow with some degree of success. These injuries have been touched on in earlier chapters, but repetition here will be nothing like the times they'll reappear in real life. The majority of debilitating injuries will occur in the joints of the knees and ankles and in the tendons. Joint problems originate from excessive pounding which usually causes the joint capsule lining to become inflamed in young horses, and the cartilage to erode, bone chips to break off or calcium deposits ("spurs") to form in the older ones.

Surgery to remove bone chips or spurs has gotten simpler, more successful and more commonplace with the introduction of arthroscopic surgery. Fiber optics allow surgeons to see inside the joint on a magnified basis so that the fleshy incisions can be very small and precise, and the tissue damage minimal. Other surgical procedures, like drilling holes and implanting screws, have been fairly reliable for simple fractures and are often followed by the popular electromagnetic therapy to promote healing. The crucial point of any operation comes when a horse first awakens from anesthesia. If he thrashes around wildly or founders from shock, you might as well kiss him goodbye.

A favorite cure-all for years was "pin-firing" or applying "blisters" to anything wrong. These were essentially primitive and painful ways of irritating tissue in order to stimulate the flow of blood to an underlying injury. Some say that you might as well fire a horse's back because what would really help the healing process most is keeping the saddle off.

Its place has been taken in recent years by "tapping," that is, removing blood and fluid from a joint and injecting cortisone. It is used with greatest success for joint capsule problems in young horses, provided you can then turn them out for a couple of months' rest. Unfortunately, the treatment's effectiveness during uninterrupted racing is fairly short-run. Relief is for two or three races at most and subsequent tappings can lead to the end of the line. The biggest drawback is that cortisone relieves the symptoms of inflammation, but does little to allay the underlying problems.

That's why the greatest hope for joint injuries has come with therapy using hyaluronic acid (HA), a substance natural to joints, but easily harvested from rooster combs and umbilical cords. It is supposed to soothe, protect and help heal like nature's equivalent to motor oil in an engine. HA has miraculously cured some horses, though not others. This points up the need for using a lab service to diagnose the stage of articular degeneration and prescribe an exact treatment. It might call for a series of HA shots, possibly in combination with substances like Arteparon or Rumalon which could help the worst cases where the cartilage is far gone.

The biggest drawback to HA therapy treatment is that it's expensive and hard to get in a pure form, and not fully blessed with government approval. Also, treatment would involve sticking needles into joints, which can be ideal spots for infections on the non-sterile backstretch.

Scientists have felt that HA has potential to alleviate arthritis in people, too. It is not unusual for humans and horses to share the same cures. Both pleasure horse people and health food junkies have always been interested in Yucca plant extract for arthritic conditions. There's even been widespread racetrack use of DMSO as a liniment for suspensory problems, which involve inflammation of the ligament sheath that splits to run down each side of a horse's foreleg near the ankles. This substance was originally popularized for bi-ped pain.

The best medicine of all is still the "tincture of time." If you give a horse with ankle problems enough time off, his joints will sometimes surprise you and "set." Neighboring tissue tries to repair itself by creating new bone mass until the whole thing seems fused together. Joints may become big, unsightly and limited in flexion, but as long as they stay cold, they'll do the job. Bad knees are a tougher nut, but time off helps there, too.

Although science is constantly advancing, there is one injury that has spelled doom for years. A "bow" pops when the tendon along the back of a horse's cannon bone becomes stretched and, in some cases, torn. At worst, the ankle drops to the ground. Heavy male horses running over a cuppy track have long been considered prime candidates for bowing. It can happen when the head, neck and shoulders rotate too far forward before the front foot is picked up, thus stretching the tendon in back of the leg beyond the bounds of elasticity.

Rest and drawing salves are the time-honored bow treatments, although new treatments are constantly on the drawing board and some seem promising. Anything with a remote chance of success—antihistamines, shots, laser beams, acupuncture—stands to make a millionaire out of its inventor. Just think: a lucky horseman in the know could slip around claiming all the wonderful horses running cheap because of bows.

The quicksand of bow treatment is getting a horse back into racing after months or years off without reinjuring the tendon. Training has to be gradual to prevent setbacks, but they seem to happen often enough anyway when push comes to shove in a workout or a race. The same pressures which caused an ugly bow in the first place can cause a horse to rebow or to develop a new injury in the same area of stress. The whole process comes packed with frustration. Examine your conscience to see if retirement isn't easier and cheaper all the way around. You will always find some horses who make it back into racing with bows, but experience says that the success rate is low for a horse to come back and even lower for him to show more than a shadow of his former ability. No odds are given on how long he'll race sound.

Some trainers actually welcome chronic bleeders into their barns because they figure that these horses will dramatically improve in class once the bleeding is controlled. They hope the problem can be helped by using a citrus complex to strengthen capillaries and female hormones to raise the level of Vitamin K for better clotting. The medication Lasix reportedly helps bleeders, but is now on the restricted list. Since Lasix has a diuretic effect, it has come under a cloud as a masker of illegal drugs, although this charge may well be unfair.

Track restrictions on bleeders are tough: horses are not allowed to run back for successively longer periods after each track-site bleeding. Yet, studies at the New Bolton Center in Pennsylvania showed that over 70% of the racehorses tested bled in their respiratory cavities, although few had bled hard enough to have blood flowing from their nostrils. The experts hedge on what causes bleeding—track dirt, thickened blood or structural weakness—and whether bleeding really affects performance.

Vets. Racetrack medicine is a mélange of the old with the new, the seemingly primitive alongside space-age technology. Whatever works is still used openly, unless specifically prohibited. Even strident proponents of going back to racing on hay, oats and water alone as a way of making the track more humane have had to acknowledge that restrictive drug legislation has led to the substitution of stronger, more harmful medicines. Because some economically hard-pressed horsemen feel driven to keep a chemical edge one hop ahead of detection technology, vets are in the hot seat.

Temptation pushes many vets into becoming needlemen, superficial Mr. Fixits. There's big money in it. Another disease that attacks both track and farm vets is big-shotitis. A fatal symptom is the disinclination to touch horses, to flex and prod, to get down on hands and knees amidst the muck and dirt and water of unknown origin. That's why you'll come to value the doctor who likes a challenge, who treats his patients with individual compassion and takes pains to explain his voodoo to the laymen standing by.

Lay-ups. Some farms specialize in "lay-ups," rest and recreation for worn-out racehorses. There's no great mystery about the process, but you'll need to have decent help. Horses coming off the track are fairly high-strung and are often suffering from injuries which need daily treatment.

The key to lay-ups is never to toss a fresh racehorse right out into a field. He'll go nuts. If he doesn't wrench something tearing around the pasture, he might eat so much fresh grass that he could founder. Put him instead in a small paddock until he gets used to the headiness of freedom. Sedate the wild ones.

SAWBONES

Dr. Foley was a hippie at heart. He didn't preach love and kindness, he lived it, morning 'til night. His beat was the racetrack, and his patients were mostly platers, the working stiffs of the racing world. These were the guys who had to hustle across the finish line to earn a bucket of oats and a bundle of hay. They knew him by sight and by touch, and this was where Foley felt most at home.

If the good doctor had a favorite barn, it had to be Lee's. It's one thing to know you're welcome with whinneys and a warm muzzle, it's another to get some real human appreciation. You could bet Lee would always be there, hanging around his tidy shedrow, hovering over the walking wounded and plying poor Doc with tough and meaty questions.

"Jesus!" thought Foley, *"Here's the first trainer who's more interested in the legs of his horses than in yakking it up over the baseball playoffs."*

Foley was still musing about it when he reached home and stuck his hand into the fridge for a beer. Goddamn! He dropped the ripening horse leg. This one had been chopped off for an insurance claim, but the adjuster turned tail and nobody else had come forward to claim the prize. Let the dogs feed elsewhere; there was no way Foley would let a pup chew on a friend. Besides, the flesh would have been poisoned by the killing shot.

Foley gently lifted the limb out and buried it in his garden with full military honors. Something had clicked, and the connection rang clear.

Foley took his time about robbing the grave until he was pretty sure the bones had been plucked clean by decay. Then he went to work on each part with a scrub brush and bleach, and by Christmas he was ready to lay the model under the tree.

When Lee pulled off the ribbon, he looked like a lost explorer being given a road map marked "home." Now he'd know exactly where to look for every fracture, chip and spur. Doc knew just how to help. He always did, even when his patients could barely stand up alone.

Success

Success is fleeting. But possible. While competing horsemen may get jealous of a successful owner, they will never feel any ill will toward a deserving horse. Horses are heroes. A good horse accepts plaudits and praise with essential indifference.

> About the head of a truly great horse there is an
> air of freedom unconquerable. The eyes seem to
> look on heights beyond our gaze. It is the look of a
> spirit that can soar. It is not confined to horses;
> even in his pictures you can see it in the eyes of
> the Bonaparte. It is the birthright of eagles.
>
> —John Taintor Foote

Racehorses are trained to run and urged to win, and the thrill of it all is reward in itself.

An unusually perceptive owner will learn dignity from the horses and affect humility in the face of success. Most of us have trouble subduing the urge to crow. Racing glory is so ephemeral that you'll be forgiven to a degree, but prolonged analyses and cute stories soon get nauseating. You might be able to captivate a stray newsman desperate for a story, but to your fellow horsemen it sounds too much like bragging. The trouble with racing is that when you are up, almost everybody else is down.

Newly successful horsemen violate established turf. It's only when they have become predominantly and indisputably successful that the awe and respect reserved for those beyond the pettiness of the everyday struggle is theirs. Racing success may turn some horsemen into legends, but in the end it's still the horses who are the stars. These people will be remembered by the grace of their best horses.

You will rarely have to tangle with bottled-up feelings—the hallmark of relations among competing owners—in your brushes with horseplayers. You'll catch hell for losing, but every bettor loves a winner.

Gambling winnings may look pale beside the purses won by horsemen, yet the equalizing factor here is that most purses are earmarked for paying bills. Win, place (first or second) or show (first, second or third) bets are pretty tame game for a hard-bitten gambler, unless he bets solid money; the standard two-dollar bet would be a joke on any odds-on favorite. When you go in for exotic bets like picking the first two or three horses across the finish line, it becomes a different ball game. Track management knows this well and has to stay up late thinking of betting schemes to toughen the challenge and sweeten the pay-off.

A healthy approach—if unrealistic—would be to consider betting losses as part of the cost of the day's entertainment. Let's face it, any pay-off probably works out to be a loan from the track. They'll get it back eventually, with interest. But dedicated gamblers don't like to think in Pollyanna terms. They are serious and single-minded, so lend them a hand. Break your own rules and dress like a slob when your horse is a rat. They'll know you didn't come for the picture.

ON GRASS

This is a story about wanting more. About how a good horse edges to the brink of greatness.

Lord Mahlon strode into a paddock with a monarch's sureness to his step and a king's quiet in his eyes. There was speed in those big ankles, which with luck were cold and set. It was only because the horse was old—not sore—that his connections felt safe in jamming him through a cheap claiming race. You see, ten grand is a lot of money anywhere but in racehorse land.

It feels so good whenever owners revile and insult you for taking their horse. You know then you've got yourself a nice little claim. Just hate to see them laughing.

Mahlon had never been challenged. We knew he was fast and he was honest. When spring came to warm his bones and give him a hard-baked track, he woke up in heaven. Given a turf course, he broke records.

The Laurel turf stake was going to be his. Easy company, hard turf. And Mahlon was hot. Felt so good that he cast himself in his stall the night before and came out of it with his stifle thrown. The race came up, the bettors laid down their lives and the stifle popped again. Doc scratched him at the gate.

The ultimate throw-up. The track lost money and we lost heart. But people recover. So they say.

♞ Chapter Eight ♞

SURVIVAL

RUNNING ON EMPTY

Bright as a penny, sparkle in the eye. Yemani was as swaybacked as they come, but still the very focus of our ambitions as the first homebred. The product of my equally swaybacked, broken-down riding horse and a half-way decent stallion.

He wasn't much, but he could have done. Won a few at a half-mile track.

Feeling the season one spring day, Yemani horsed around until the exercise yoke caught under his armpit and rubbed it raw. The wound was ugly and deep in a tortuous spot.

Nine months later we greeted the returning prodigal son, healed and ready to run. Gave him a race, then another, easier still. Nada.

"She's cheating on you, mon," said the jock. *"This is one horse that's too smart to run."*

Yemani disappeared into the gypsy world of the fair circuit. The race-horse pits. Last I heard they used an electric gator on him, and he went through the rail. There's just one more stop on this line because the leisure market likes a looker. Not a swaybacked drop-out.

ATTITUDES

Whenever enthusiasm dies, it's time to count your money and watch it grow in tamer ventures. As it is, most horsemen suffer from an idiot's surplus of the stuff. The maturation process of a horse is relatively short, but it still leaves plenty of time for horsemen to daydream over a foal of promise. Yet unlike human children whose troubles can be counted on to drag out over a lifetime of 60 years or more, a horse's racing career will be telescoped into a few years at most.

Hope

Make yourself look beyond the present generation of horses to the upcoming ranks of two-year-olds, yearlings and weanlings if you ever need a reason to smile. Even their problems will be refreshingly new. Renewal of hope is racing's secret, and it will keep you young.

The *RACING FORM* is itself incentive to get out of bed. The only real antidote for a horse that's doing badly is one that's doing well, and lacking that, claiming races hold out the chance for a quick cure. Whenever you feel the hunter's blood coursing through your veins, go after a claim with cunning and conviction. Be impassioned. Never claim just another horse to fill a slot. By the same token, don't allow yourself to mourn a good claim that got away. With horses as with lovers, there are many more fish in the sea.

Enthusiasm will be disastrous only if you insist that everyone both in and out of racing has to share in your delight. Put away those smudged snapshots. To John Q. Public, grandchildren and horses look exhaustingly alike. Track etiquette says that a bore must be listened to only enough for you to claim equal time to bore him back. That's just so long as he doesn't talk during a race.

Remind yourself that the only proof of a good racehorse is his win record on the track. It never quite washes when you explain or excuse a milksop effort. Of course every race has a story—the saddle slipped, the jock lost his whip. Save all your "coulda-shoulda-wouldas" for your trainer; he's being paid as a shoulder to cry on. If you share in the management of your horses, though, you've got to take on some of the blame when things go wrong.

The vision of gathering your laurels in front of admiring friends and family is chimerical. No horse can take that kind of pressure. What's more, crucial races are particularly hard on guests. Give them some groundschool on how to treat a major racing reversal: ignore it, lay low. Attempts at sympathy or cheeriness do not fly. The world's end will eventually pass, and numbness will be chased by anger and hope. But the fact remains that, in the superstitious and unfair world of racing, all guests are fair game for blame.

Owners are in the limelight, they belong to racing's public. While most people must be content to see their names in print only in the phone book, worthy owners will be written up regularly and can become more immediately recognizable than a network sportscaster within the racetrack community. Wear it well. No need for spats and a cane, just be distinguishable from your groom. Racing has an old world flavor which conjures up women in hats and diaphanous gowns, so save the gold lamé jumpsuit for the supermarket. And never let your thoughts stray to how dapper you'll look in the winning picture. Bad joss. Dress for the race, not for the win.

Realism

The American public is now being pleasantly spoiled by 24-hour grocery stores, all-night TV and being able to go racing just about any time. Pity the rest of the world which must content itself with short meets, frugally dispersed. But save some of your pity for horses in ruthless barns who may be forced to race more often than horse sense prescribes. Drugs are an inadequate substitute for R&R.

As for self-pity, you're in the wrong business. Luck can be a tough and emancipated lady. She needs no excuse to crunch you under her heel. As long as track officials outdo themselves to perpetuate an aura of racing honesty, especially at the smaller tracks, you can eventually learn to live with your luck without question or bitterness.

It's always difficult to pinpoint a dishonest ride since accidents and incompetency are to be expected, especially with jockeys you don't often use. If your suspicions are awfully strong, you should diplomatically ask the stewards to review the race. Otherwise, keep your opinions to yourself, swallow your rage and be content never to ride that jock again. No point in starting a vendetta.

You can't expect racing to be kind. The heavens toy mercilessly with the aspirations of every horseman and horseplayer. Racing variables that can go wrong are infinite. Don't bother to bank on the race which seems to be shaping up perfectly in every way; conversely, it does no good to imagine everything that can go wrong has gone wrong. Why be a chump?

You might also expect racing to have a sense of compensating balance. Never. Problems on the track invariably coincide with those at home and in business. Racing is such a personal sport that the well-being of your racing stable becomes an integral part of your life. That's why it's a direct reflection of class to earn the label "smart barn." With the emphasis on "earn."

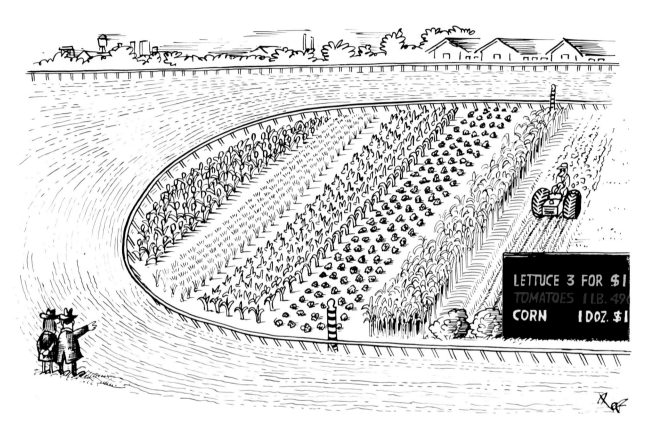

'THIS EXPERIMENT WAS AUTHORIZED BY THE STATE LEGISLATURE TO HELP INCREASE OUR PURSE DISTRIBUTION.'

ECONOMICS

A rough ride for owners is dancing school patter compared to the bloody competition going on among tracks for the public's gambling dollar. States are hard-pressed for tax revenue and are granting longer meets so that racetrackers can often choose between several tracks operating simultaneously in one region. Every track tries hard to attract quality racing outfits to draw in more betting fans, but the dropout rate of bankrupt stables shows that purses can rarely be boosted high enough to keep pace with expenses. As a compensation for surviving, owners are often treated to attractive conditions, short fields and an accommodating management, if not more money.

On the whole, racetracks have risen valiantly to meet the challenge of wooing the public. Lining up corporations to sponsor races is one way to stretch money for purses. The biggest coup in years was the inauguration of the Budweiser Million—this country's first million dollar Thoroughbred race—held at Chicago's Arlington Park. Talk first circulated that Bud would get more publicity out of its Clydesdales than the race and that some of the more nondescript starters might be inclined to lounge to the competitor's tune, "When it's time to relax . . . ." On the bright side, though, this race has given Arlington Park a new track record, a day of top attendance and all-important popular recognition.

PR men continue the struggle to schedule big name concerts, closed-circuit boxing matches and giant giveaways—just about anything to draw in new racing fans. These activities can sometimes backlash to scare off the more serious horseplayers who tend to run from amateur crowds, but most racetracks are built roomy enough to accommodate the world with some foresight and planning.

Pimlico's General Manager, Chick Lang, is a hero in the land of PR. Capable and colorful, Chick's aim in life has been to promote the Preakness Stakes onto the glittering plane of the Kentucky Derby. Preakness Week has its queen, games, prizes and exceptional racing cards. Preakness Day may be standing room only in the Clubhouse, but everybody's welcome in the infield circus.

OTB or Not To Be.

Racetrack accountants seem to be putting most of their faith in off-track-betting (OTB) as a highly effective way of bringing home the bacon. Discussions of OTB are complicated by the fact that this is a new field where words are continually being coined for offshoots of the same thing; innovations and the language have not yet jelled. Every locality seems to have its own home-grown hybrid for making more money through the broadcasting and betting on races off-track.

Critics claim that New York's pioneering OTB system was devised in a slap-dash and single-minded attempt to improve government solvency at the cost of undercutting the handle at the tracks. That's why many horsemen are extremely wary of it, even though OTB shops have managed to co-exist for years with on-track parimutuel facilities all around the world.

In 1983, New York operated a statewide program of about 300 betting parlors, with 134 located in New York City proper. The shops were purposely austere so that they would not compete with on-track amenities. In fact, New York law at that time wouldn't allow regular closed-circuit televised races known as simulcasts. (These have always been in existence next door in Connecticut's tele-theater operation, "Teletrack," which has never had to worry about contending with instate racing.) The New York shops did come equipped with a TV odds board, though, and some even carried the call of the race. A private line was set up for dialing race results, while every Saturday night OTB broadcast a program on local television showing the feature race as well as one other from Saturday's card. The money rolled in.

Horsemen have been successful in persuading the authorities that turning back a larger share of the take to the tracks, and earmarking it for track improvement and larger purses, would pay off royally for everyone. Substantial purses and first class facilities should help attract top flight horses, which are the strongest drawing card for both the on- and off-track betting fans. A little spit and polish can always be counted on to pull more fans into the racetracks. That's because—no matter what—an OTB parlor is a pale substitute for the horses and all the rainbow colors of the racing world.

Götterdämmerung

"They're in the gate.
"The flag is up . . . .
"And they're off!"

With a jump and a stride, Seattle Slew flashed to the front and drew away from the field. But no lengths could dull the relentless Secretariat stalking in back: Big Red ran easy, had power to spare. In the far turn, he started making his move, sweeping out wide to gun down the pack in its tracks.

Lumbering far back and mid-track, Forego's big heart caught fire at the sight of the stretch. This was Forego-land, a runway for jets.

"They're gonna run today!"

Slew pinned his ears and drove on with courage as Sexy thundered into view, thrusting the power of his stallion's crest into every fiery stride. Then came time for cool hand "Shoe" on the giant horse to twitch a muscle and pop his stick. No need—old Forego had already flattened out to hurl all seventeen hands. And that's when the track dirt flew.

"Lookout, folks, they're rolling! It's Seattle Slew by a head! Now Secretariat's gaining the lead . . . no, it's Forego!"

Three noses whipped in fury right down to the wire. Head-to-head and matching strides, red and brown blurred into one straining silhouette of sinew and sweat. They swept past the finish line the way they'd exploded from the gate—the circuit was completed, in unison and in style.

It never happened, but the world would have stopped to watch. To own any part of this greatness, even a half-sister to the fourth dam, is what keeps you going. And yet who can say why such things are important, and why some creatures will live on in your heart long after you've seen them run.

'NOW I REMEMBER: I WAS ON SUNSHOT THAT DAY AND YOU WERE RIDING GREY HAWK!'

CONCLUSIONS

Horsemen may be unlucky, but they are rarely daunted. Lost races have their twice-told tales. Every fool has an excuse. Or ten.

The world should go easy on horsemen and try not to prick the bubble of their involvement. A little craziness makes life fun. Racing is an ever-ready source of conversation sure to interest and revive a horseman's libido as powerfully as any aphrodisiac.

Although a life-time of racing may also introduce its share of hair-tearing misery into your life, it is tailor-made for those who need the sharp edge of passion to convince themselves that they are fully alive. Passion is there all right, and an owner will be treated to it—the exhilaration and the pain—both as a spectator and as a participant. Other problems will shrink commensurately; there's little time left for mid-life handwringing, much less for brooding about the serious and depressing problems of the outside world.

Racing's big appeal is that it reduces the world to basics. There's a winner in every race. Real life isn't this sporting: it is a morass of maybe's where the occasional triumph may seem anticlimatic. Despite the temptation to redboard and grouse, horsemen will always know which horse won what race at the end of each racing card.

You'll have to grow a few callouses to survive in racing. The sport has moments of brutality and bitterness, although few horsemen could be called heartless. Racing wisdom comes hard-fought every day. Local in origin, but universal in application. You can take it with you to any track, anywhere.

Your racing stable will help you override the relentless process of growing up, becoming old and respectable. The racing world never stands still long enough to dull your wits, and the scent of success is a powerful draw. There will always be talented new horses coming into your life to refresh your spirit and fill you with great hope.

@*#!!

APPENDICES

Appendix I

Relative Purse Value

The following table may be used as an adjunct to Daily Racing Form's past performance feature of showing the value of allowance race purses. The number in bold face type following the name of each track (except hunt meets) represents the average net purse value per race (including stakes and overnight races), rounded to the nearest thousand, during the track's 1982 season. A comparison thus can be made of the value of an allowance purse in a horse's current past performances with the average value of all races at that track the preceding season. The purse value index in the track abbreviation table will be changed each year to reflect the values of the previous season. If no purse value index is shown in the following table, the track did not operate a race meeting last year.

AC   — (Agua) Caliente, Mexico—**3**
Aks — Ak-Sar-Ben, Neb.—**10**
Alb — *Albuquerque, N. Mex.—**7**
AP   — Arlington Park, Ill.—**11**
Aqu — Aqueduct, N.Y.—**20**
AsD — *Assiniboia Downs, Canada—**4**
Atl — Atlantic City, N.J.—**7**
Ato — *Atokad Park, Neb.—**1**
BD   — *Berkshire Downs, Mass.
Bel — Belmont Park, N.Y.—**25**
Beu — Beulah Race Track, Ohio—**4**
Bil — *Billings, Mont.—**1**
BM   — Bay Meadows, Cal.—**11**
Bmf — Bay Meadows Fair, Cal.—**10**
Bml — Balmoral Park, Ill.—**3**
Boi — *Boise, Idaho—**1**
Bow — Bowie, Md.—**9**
CD   — Churchill Downs, Ky.—**12**
Cda — *Coeur d'Alene, Idaho—**1**
Cen — Centennial Race Track, Colo.—**2**
Cka — *Cahokia Downs, Ill.
Cls — *Columbus, Neb.—**2**
Com — *Commodore Downs, Pa.—**2**
Crc — Calder Race Course, Fla.—**9**
CT   — *Charles Town, W. Va.—**3**
Dar — *Darby Downs, Ohio—**4**
        (Formerly Beulah Race Track)
DeD — *Delta Downs, La.—**3**
Del — Delaware Park, Del.—**8**
Det — Detroit Race Course, Mich.—**5**
Dmr — Del Mar, Cal.—**19**
Dmf — Del Mar Fair, Cal.—**9**
Elm — *Elma, Wash.
EIP — Ellis Park, Ky.—**5**
EnP — †Enoch Park, Canada
EP   — *Exhibition Park, Canada—**6**
EvD — *Evangeline Downs, La.—**4**
FD   — Florida Downs, Fla.
FE   — Fort Erie, Canada—**7**
Fer — *Ferndale, Cal.—**1**
FG   — Fair Grounds, La.—**10**.
FL   — Finger Lakes, N.Y.—**5**
Fno — Fresno, Cal.—**4**
Fon — *Fonner Park, Neb.—**3**
FP   — Fairmount Park, Ill.—**4**
GBF — *Great Barrington, Mass.—**2**
GD   — †Galway Downs, Cal.
GF   — *Great Falls, Mont.—**1**
GG   — Golden Gate Fields, Cal.—**11**
GP   — Gulfstream Park, Fla.—**12**
Grd — *Greenwood, Canada—**10**

GrP — *Grants Pass, Ore.—**1**
GS   — †Garden State Park, N. J.
Haw — Hawthorne, Ill.—**10**
Hia — Hialeah Park, Fla.—**13**
Hol — Hollywood Park, Cal.—**25**
HP   — *Hazel Park, Mich.—**6**
Imp — *Imperial, Cal.
JnD — *Jefferson Downs, La.—**5**
Jua — Juarez, Mexico
Kee — Keeneland, Ky.—**17**
Key — Keystone Race Track, Pa.—**8**
LA   — *Los Alamitos, Cal.—**10**
LaD — Louisiana Downs, La.—**13**
LaM — *La Mesa Park, N. Mex.—**2**
Lar — Nuevo Laredo, Mexico
Lat — Latonia, Ky.—**4**
Lbg — *Lethbridge, Canada
Lga — Longacres, Wash.—**6**
LnN — *Lincoln State Fair, Neb.—**4**
Lrl — Laurel Race Course, Md.—**9**
MD   — *Marquis Downs, Canada—**2**
Med — Meadowlands, N.J.—**13**
Mex — *Mexico City, Mexico
MF   — *Marshfield Fair, Mass.—**2**
Mth — Monmouth Park, N. J.—**10**
Nmp — *Northampton, Mass.—**2**
NP   — *Northlands Park, Canada—**5**
OP   — Oaklawn Park, Ark.—**14**
OTC — †Ocala Training Center, Fla.
Pay — †Payson Park, Fla.
Pen — Penn National, Pa.—**4**
Pim — Pimlico, Md.—**11**
PJ   — *Park Jefferson, S. D.—**1**
Pla — *Playfair, Wash.—**2**
Pln — Pleasanton, Cal.—**8**
PM   — Portland Meadows, Ore.—**3**
Pmf — Portl'nd M'd'ws Fair, Ore.
Poc — *Pocono Downs, Pa.
Pom — *Pomona, Cal.—**12**
PR   — Puerto Rico (El Com'te)
Pre — *Prescott Downs, Ariz.—**1**
Rap — *Rapid City, S.D.
RD   — River Downs, Ohio—**4**
Reg — *Regina, Canada—**2**
Ril — *Rillito, Ariz.—**1**
Rkm — Rockingham Park, N. H.
Rui — *Ruidoso, N. Mex.—**4**
SA   — Santa Anita Park, Cal.—**26**
Sac — Sacramento, Cal.—**5**
Sal — *Salem, Ore. (Lone Oak)—**1**
San — *Sandown Park, Canada—**2**

Sar — Saratoga, N.Y.—**26**
SFe — *Santa Fe, N. Mex.—**3**
ShD — †*Shenand'h Downs, W. Va.
SLR — †San Luis Rey Downs, Cal.
Sol — *Solano, Cal.—**6**
Spt — *Sportsman's Park, Ill.—**11**
SR   — *Santa Rosa, Cal. —**6**
Stk — Stockton, Cal.—**5**
StP — *Stampede Park, Canada—**5**
Suf — Suffolk Downs, Mass.—**6**
SuD — *Sun Downs, Wash.—**1**
Sun — Sunland Park, N. Mex.—**3**
Tam — Tampa Bay Downs, Fla.—**3**
        (Formerly Florida Downs)
Tdn — Thistledown, Ohio—**4**
Tim — *Timonium, Md.—**5**
TuP — Turf Paradise, Ariz.—**3**
Vic — *Victorville, Cal.
Was — Washington Park, Ill.
Wat — Waterford Park, W. Va.—**2**
WO   — Woodbine, Canada—**13**
YM   — Yakima Meadows, Wash.—**1**

HUNT MEETINGS

Aik — Aiken, S. Carolina
AtH — Atlanta, Ga.
Cam — Camden, S. Carolina
Clm — Clemmons, N. Carolina
Fai — Fair Hill, Md.
Fax — Fairfax, Va.
FH   — Far Hills, N. J.
Fx   — Foxfield, Va.
Gln — Glyndon, Md.
GN   — *Grand National, Md.
Lex — Lexington, Ky.
Lig — Ligonier, Pa.
Mal — Malvern, Pa.
Mid — Middleburg, Va.
Mon — Monkton, Md.
Mor — Morven Park, Va.
Mtp — Montpelier, Va.
Oxm — Oxmoor, Ky.
Pro — Prospect, Ky.
PW   — Percy Warner, Tenn.
RB   — Red Bank, N. J.
SH   — Strawberry Hill, Va.
SoP — Southern Pines, N. C.
Try — Tryon, N.C.
Uni — Unionville, Pa
War — Warrenton, Va
Wel — Wellsville, Pa.

Tracks marked with (*) are less than one mile in circumference. †Training facility only.

Appendix II

Chapter Three-**Weaning**

The Sign Calendar

AUGUST 1983						
S	**M**	**T**	**W**	**T**	**F**	**S**
	1	2	3	4	5	6
7	8	9	10	11	12	13
14	15	16	17	18	♐	20
21	22	23	24	25	♈	27
28	29	30	31			

THE "SIGN" IN AUGUST

2	♉	Neck	16	♐	Thighs
4	♊	Arms	19	♑	Knees
6	♋	Breast	21	♒	Legs
8	♌	Heart	24	♓	Feet
10	♍	Bowels	26	♈	Head
12	♎	Kidneys	29	♉	Neck
14	♏	Loins	31	♊	Arms

—Courtesy of THE BLOOD-HORSE

Appendix III

Chapter Three-**Home Care**

Medical Records

Year: _____

Horse: _____

Birthdate: _____

	Last Date in previous Year	JAN	FEB	MAR	APR	MAY	JUNE	JULY	AUG	SEPT	OCT	NOV	DEC
1. Blacksmith													
2. Worming													
3. Shots a) Tetanus													
b) Equine Influenza													
c) Rhinopneumonitis													
d) Encephalomyelitis													
e) Rabies													
f) Other													
4. Coggins Test													
5. Dental Work													

Appendix IV

Chapter Three-**Names**

Naming a Thoroughbred

Naming a thoroughbred is not the simple process as it might seem. Names submitted by owners must conform to the rules and regulations set forth by The Jockey Club and must be approved by their Stewards. Names are limited to 18 letters (spaces and punctuation marks count as letters) with no limitation on the number of words.

Names that have been used during the previous 15 years, either in the stud or in racing, cannot be duplicated and names cannot be claimed for unregistered horses, although those which are eligible may be reserved for one year. Names of stallions whose daughters are in stud, names of famous or notorious persons and trade names or names of commercial significance are not acceptable. Names which bear any suggestive, vulgar or obscene meaning are prohibited. Identical prefixes or suffixes may not be used by any owner in naming horses bred or owned by him. The usage of 2nd, 3rd, etc., even though spelled out, may not be used in names.

Names of famous horses and names whose spelling or pronunciation are similar to those already used are restricted. Copyrighted names (titles of books, songs, movies, etc.) may be used five years after those names were first introduced. Names of living persons are allowed only if written permission is filed with The Jockey Club, individually, by the persons whose names are to be used. When foreign words or names are requested, an English translation must be furnished. "Coined" or "made-up" names must be accompanied with an explanation. An owner may change the name of a horse prior to January 1 of the 2-year-old year. After that date permission must be granted by the Stewards of The Jockey Club. However, no change will be permitted after a horse has started.

Owners usually submit additional names as alternates in case their first choice is not approved. Some owners combine a part of the sire's name with that of the mare's in naming thoroughbreds. The late Col. E. R. Bradley gave his horses names beginning with the letter "B." Brookfield Farm has used "I" as the first letter in naming its thoroughbreds.

Appendix V

Chapter Five–**Auctions**

Sales Catalog Pedigree

Hip No.   Property of Golden Rose Thoroughbreds,
139   James W. Hechter, Agent

Bay Filly

Half-sister to Tom's Rule (5 wins to 4, 1979, $17,300). Out of RUN FOR TOM (10 wins, Senorita S., etc.), half-sister to stakes-placed Fasteddy, Montana Flyer. Second dam half-sister to PRINCE QUEST (3 wins, $48,485), stakes-placed Lucky Reward.

Bay Filly April 17, 1978	Rollicking	Rambunctious	*Rasper II / *Danae II
		Martinetta	Martins Rullah / Gracefield
	Run for Tom (1968)	Run for Nurse	Hasty Road / Juliets Nurse
		Darksteddy	Dark Star / Teddys Queen

By ROLLICKING (1967), stakes winner of 14 races, $196,396. Sire of stakes winners Danger Bearing (8 wins to 4, 1979, $134,968, Cameo S., etc.), Rock'n Rollick (4 wins to 3, 1979, $83,678, E. Palmer Heagerty S., etc.), Call the King, Enthused, etc.

1st dam
RUN FOR TOM, by Run for Nurse. 10 wins, 2 to 6, $28,186, Senorita S., 3rd
    Raton Derby. This is her fourth foal. Dam of 2 foals to race—
    Tom's Rule (c. by Final Ruling). 5 wins at 3 and 4, 1979, $17,300.
    Mercy Flite (f. by North Flight). Winner at 3, 1980, $4,400.

2nd dam
DARKSTEDDY, by Dark Star. Placed at 2. Dam of 9 foals to race, 8 winners,
    including—
    RUN FOR TOM (Run for Nurse). Stakes winner, see above.
    Fasteddy. 7 wins, 2 to 4, 2nd Mescalero-Apache H., Memorial Day H., 3rd
    Arizona Derby, Inaugural H., etc. Sire.
    Montana Flyer. 4 wins, 3rd Fleur de Lis S. Producer.
    Dark Heritage. 6 wins, 2 to 5, $22,156.

3rd dam
TEDDYS QUEEN, by *Teddy. Winner at 2 and 3. Half-sister to **Exalted Ruler.**
    Produced 5 winners, including—
    PRINCE QUEST. 3 wins at 2, $48,485, Ardsley H., Great American S., 3rd
    East View S., Wakefield S. Sire.
    Lucky Reward. 8 wins, 2 to 5, $22,080, 3rd Wakefield S., Sanford S.
    Tante Florence. Winner at 3. Producer.
    Pillow Lecture. Unraced. Dam of 3 winners, including—
      TODO CORAZON. 9 wins, Mescalero Apache H., Inaugural H., 2nd
      Santa Fe H., Inaugural H., 3rd El Paso H. Sire.
      Duchess Keady. Winner at 2. Dam of **PSYCHIC KNOT** (10 wins,
      $53,976, Littletown Futurity, etc.), **NEKE JR.** (7 wins, $49,504,
      Phoenix Futurity, etc.), **MAXITO, Alliance Royal** (to 4, 1980).
      Kitchy Koo. Dam of **PEACEFUL REQUEST** (11 wins, $51,769, New
      Mexico Thoroughbred Futurity, etc.), **Peaceful Lecture.**
    Mary Adelle. Unraced. Dam of **TAITSUBAKI** (Hanshin Fillies Special H. in
    Japan). Granddam of **TOORU** (in Japan).

Registered Maryland-bred.
                                                3-80

—Courtesy of the Maryland Horse Breeders Association

Picture the Pedigree

Sire: Hot. A dandy stallion, big locally. Consistent. Keeps on throwing stakes winners.

This means that the filly has a fallback position of good broodmare potential. Breeders will figure that the sire's talent is in her blood even if it decides to skip a generation or so.

Bottom Line: The black type's there and lots of it. From mom to great grandma. Stakes winners are printed bold-face, stakes-placed horses in lower-case black type. But look carefully. Some of those races look like small purses, southwestern tracks. Not exactly Group I even if it catalogs well.

Siblings: They didn't set the world on fire, but they won a few. Their sires were decent, which means that the mare's owner had confidence in her.

Birth Place: Everybody likes to see a registered state-bred. Opens doors and improves purses. Shows the local involvement of the breeders. They are not likely to be fly-by-night.

Appendix VI

Chapter Five-**How to Milk the *RACING FORM***

HOW SPEED RATINGS ARE COMPUTED

The Speed Rating is a comparison of the horse's final time with the track record established prior to the opening of the meeting. The track record is given a rating of 100. One point is deducted for each fifth of a second by which a horse fails to equal the track record (one length is approximately equal to one-fifth of a second). Thus, in a race in which the winner equals the track record (a Speed Rating of 100), another horse who is beaten 12 lengths (or an estimated two and two-fifths seconds) receives a Speed Rating of 88 (100 minus 12). If a horse breaks the track record he receives an additional point for each one-fifth second by which he lowers the record (if the track record is 1:10 and he is timed in 1:09⅗, his Speed Rating is 102).

NOTE: In computing beaten-off distances for Speed Ratings, fractions of one-half length or more are figured as one full length (one point). No Speed Ratings are given for steeplechase or hurdle events, for races of less than three furlongs, or for races for which the Speed Rating would be less than 25.

When Daily Racing Form prints its own time, in addition to the official track time, the Speed Rating is based on the official track time. Speed Ratings for new distances at a track are computed and assigned when adequate time standards are established.

HOW TRACK VARIANTS ARE COMPUTED

The Track Variant takes into consideration all of the races on a particular day and could reflect either the quality of the competition, how many points below par the track happened to be, or both. The Speed Rating of each winner is added together, then an average is taken based on the number of races run. This average is deducted from the track par of 100 and the difference is the Track Variant (example: average Speed Rating of winners involved is 86; par is 100; the Track Variant is 14). When there is a change in the track condition during the course of a program the following procedure is employed in compiling the Variant: races run on dirt tracks classified as fast, frozen or good, and those listed as hard, firm or good on the turf, are used in striking one average. Strips classified as slow, sloppy, muddy or heavy on the dirt, or yielding and soft on the turf, are grouped for another average. If all the races on a program are run in either one or the other of these general classifications, only one average is used. The lower the variant the faster the track, or the better the overall quality of the competition.

NOTE: A spearate Track Variant is computed for races run on the turf (grass), straight course races, and for races run around turns at a distance of less than 5 furlongs.